The American Alps

The American

Donald L. Baars

Alps

The San Juan Mountains of Southwest Colorado

University of New Mexico Press
Albuquerque

Library of Congress Cataloging-in-Publication Data
Baars, Donald L.
    The American Alps : the San Juan Mountains of Southwest
Colorado / Donald L. Baars. — 1st ed.
        p.   cm.
    Includes index.
    ISBN 0–8263–1352–3
    1. Geology—San Juan Mountains (Colo. and N.M.)   2. San
Juan Mountains (Colo. and N.M.)—Description and travel.
3. Geology—San Juan Mountains (Colo. and N.M.)—Guidebooks.
I. Title.
QE92.S3B33   1992
557.88′3—dc20   92–8859
                                                                        CIP

Contents

Introduction

Without a doubt, the San Juan Mountains, nestled in southwestern Colorado, are the most alpine, scenic, and geologically fascinating ranges in the southern Rocky Mountains province. Mountaineers have thrilled to the lofty peaks and crags for decades, fishermen have harvested the lakes and rills for even longer, and prospectors have ravaged the mountains for gold, silver, and other metallic riches for more than a century. Now, ever-increasing numbers of tourists threaten to devour the beauty of the American Alps. Long before this alpine paradise was discovered by twentieth-century adventurers, the Native Americans, principally the Ute and Navajo Indians, roamed the high country in search of bear, elk, deer, mountain sheep, and other, smaller game.

Why is this magnificent upland unique? Everyone has a different answer based on their perspective. Merchants of rods and reels, rifles, and camping gear believe it is the basic instinct of mankind to get back to nature, to hunt and fish for one's natural food supply, to fight for survival as our ancestors did. Nowhere in the southern Rockies offers more pristine lands than these. Prospectors who crossed the rocky ridges and dug holes in every exposure of red rock and dirt believed the land was meant to provide riches for those with prospecting prowess. Untold riches have been found and lost in the San Juans. To the restless Ute (pronounced "yoot") Indian, these mountains represented an abundant food supply.

The miracle of the San Juan Mountains has resulted from more than two billion years of geologic processes and forces. It has taken all of geologic history, perhaps as much as four billion years, to render this part of Planet Earth into huge broken basins and uplifts, to deposit a blanket of sedimentary rock more than three miles thick, to bulge the rock layers into a gigantic rounded dome, to spew forth several thousand feet of volcanic lavas and ash, and finally to sculpt the upland surface into myriad ragged crags, rounded valleys, and deep canyons by the relentless scouring of glaciers and roaring mountain rivers, to form the landscape we know and love today. Not only geologists but anyone with a whit of curiosity and a little help in understanding geologic processes and endless geologic time can learn to appreciate this alpine wilderness called the American Alps.

To appreciate the geologic history of the San Juan Mountains in terms we can all understand, this book is divided into two parts.

Part One is a primer of the many geologic processes that resulted in today's landscape in southwestern Colorado. It will take us back to the very beginnings of time insofar as can be determined and view the pages of the book of geologic happenings that forged the land. As John Wesley Powell wrote of the Grand Canyon in 1875, " . . . the book is open and we can read as we run." Finally, we will examine human involvement with the geologic masterpiece of the San Juan Mountains.

Part Two is a geologic tour guide that explains the present-day terrain most accessible by road, rail, and trail. The geology along the main paved highways, especially the San Juan Skyway, and the narrow-gauge railroad are described, and geologic aspects of the many mountaineering destinations are explained. This second part may be used separately for purposes of touring the country, especially for those with a rudimentary understanding of geologic principles, but the complex geologic history of the region is not duplicated in this section.

I wish to express special thanks to C.M. "K" Molenaar, who shared many of my climbing and geologic activities in the San Juan Mountains, and who made numerous corrections and constructive suggestions in the preparation of this book. Paul See was an inspiring accomplice during the early geological work that led to the interpretation of the complex geology of the San Juan Mountains; his efforts and presence were especially rewarding. Finally, editorial suggestions by Rex Buchanan have greatly improved the manuscript and are much appreciated.

Part One
Geology

Chapter 1

Some Basics

Geographic Setting

The San Juan Mountains dominate southwestern Colorado. Elevations range from 6,000 feet to 14 summits that exceed 14,000 feet; hundreds of peaks rise above 12,000 feet. Timberline occurs at between 11,000 and 11,500 feet, therefore much of the lofty terrain is barren, rocky, and inhospitable to most forms of life. Below timberline, however, lush stands of pine, fir, and aspen host a variety of animal life.

Heavy summer thunderstorms and winter snows provide ample moisture to the high country, but rare, torrential autumn rains can be devastating. As the highland is first in line to receive the prevailing southwesterly winds and storms that cross hundreds of miles of desert, it is the primary focus of precipitation in the southern Rocky Mountains. Snow accumulations in the high passes often exceed 100 inches, with Wolf Creek Pass recording the deepest snow pack in Colorado, sometimes nearly 200 inches. It is not surprising that the San Juan Mountains were heavily glaciated during the Ice Ages of the past million years.

Drainage patterns are radial from the roughly circular uplift. The San Juan River drains the southeastern quadrant of the mountain range, with its headwaters near Wolf Creek Pass northeast of Pagosa Springs. Farther west the smaller Pine and Piedra rivers relieve the region around the high Needles Mountains. Another major tributary, the Animas River (historically named El Rio de las Animas Perdidas—the River of Lost Souls), gathers runoff from the high central San Juan Mountains around Silverton. The Animas joins the San Juan River in northern New Mexico and eventually flows into the Colorado River. The confluence of the San Juan and Colorado rivers is now inundated by man-made Lake Powell.

On the west, the Dolores River originates in the high country above Rico and Lizard Head Pass and flows southwestward through Dolores, Colorado. It would seem logical for the Dolores to flow southwest and join the San Juan River, but instead, by a complex set of circumstances, it wanders erratically northward through western Colorado to join the Colorado River between Grand Junction and Moab, Utah. The San Miguel and Uncompahgre (pronounced "un-come-pah!-gray") rivers drain the northwestern and northern quadrants of the range, eventually joining the Dolores and Gunnison rivers, respectively.

As the Continental Divide generally bisects the San Juan Mountains, the Rio Grande and its tributaries carry runoff from the eastern San Juan Mountains on the long journey to the Gulf of Mexico.

The mountains are subdivided into several ranges, named individually as physiographic entities. The Needles, Grenadiers, Silverton, and Sneffels ranges contain peaks that are truly alpine. Each range is unique, with varying topographic style and geologic significance. One range, the Needles, is made of granite; another, the Grenadiers, consists of highly contorted and upturned quartzite layers; others have been carved by ancient glaciers out of volcanic rock. Together, in random combination, the ranges form the alpine massif known as the San Juan Mountains. Because of the myriad rugged peaks, the varied mountainous terrain, and the complex geologic relationships, they are sometimes appropriately called the American Alps.

Historical Geography

Villages and towns in and adjacent to the San Juan Mountains were originally located to serve the needs of the mining industry. Travel routes, the highways and railroads, were built to serve the logistical needs of nineteenth-century miners. Durango, first named Animas City, was a natural focal point for mining activities. It is located at the south margin of the high country, where the climate is more hospitable for year-round activities, and access to and from the mountains was reasonably easy. Wagon trails were built over game and Indian trails in the early stages of mineral prospecting. A railroad was later built northward along the Animas River Valley and then through its deep, rugged canyon leading to Silverton, which was the hub of mining activity. The narrow-gauge train carried mining equipment and supplies to Silverton and ore back to a smelter at Durango. Ore shipment was all downhill, and only the mineral concentrates had to be shipped from Durango by rail to Denver and Pueblo markets.

Another narrow-gauge railroad was built to connect Durango with the developing mines at Ophir (pronounced "oh!-fur") and Telluride (pronounced "tell!-your-ride") in the western San Juans. The engines on this line were trucks mounted on railroad wheels, and the train was known as the Galloping Goose. Mines in the northern San Juans (Red Mountain, Ironton Park, and the Sneffels districts) were supplied through Ouray (pronounced "your!-ray" in southwestern Colorado, "oh!-ray" in northern Utah) at the northern fringe of the mountains. Creede and Lake City served miners to the east. As wagon trails gradually were built to connect these major supply points, the present-day road network was established. Modern highways, although tortuous in places and plagued by avalanches in winter, now replace the original network of trails and serve the region well.

Geologic Setting

Mountaineering and geology are closely related phenomena. In the early days, many of the principles of geology resulted directly from the curiosity of climbers. They wondered how mountains were shaped, how the various types of rock were formed, why some rock layers lie flat while others are upturned and crumpled, and most importantly, how and why mountains are formed at all. This curiosity is aroused because the rocks are usually well exposed, especially in the harsh climates of high mountains, and features of the rocks are displayed beautifully as nowhere else. The San Juan Mountains are a mountaineer's mecca, attracting climbers from around the world, and the complex geologic relationships found here arouse anyone's curiosity. Indeed, these complexities have created the excellent climbing conditions, and in return, mountaineering geologists have solved many geological problems by studying these rocks.

Geological forces arched the originally flat-lying rocks upward into a huge dome, raising the earth's crust high into the realm of severe erosional processes in the San Juan Mountains. Since the dome was formed, some 65 million years ago, erosion has removed the upper layers, exposing the core of the dome. Geologists call the older, usually crystalline rocks beneath the sedimentary cover the *basement*, and these mountains offer a rare opportunity to view basement rocks. Raging mountain streams have been responsible for much of the erosional destruction, but glacial ice has carved horn-shaped peaks, scraped out U-shaped valleys, and deposited the resulting debris on surrounding lowlands during the past million years. With much of the remaining highlands still near or above timberline, where soil and vegetation cannot hide the rocks, they are laid bare for study. And what a geological showcase has resulted! The San Juan Mountains are one of the finest natural geological laboratories in existence.

It is fortuitous that uplift occurred precisely here, as the location is at the intersection of two important geological and physiographic provinces, the Colorado Plateau and the Rocky Mountains. Indeed, geographers place the San Juan Mountains in the southern Rocky Mountains province, because they certainly are rocky mountains. However, most geologists would include the San Juans in the Colorado Plateau because of geological similarities. In either case, the innermost secrets of geologic history have been revealed here.

Exposure of the oldest basement rocks, dating back to about two billion years, has revealed the presence and timing of a continental-scale fault system (fractures in the earth's crust along which movement has occurred) that extend northwestward at least from central Oklahoma diagonally across southwestern Colorado and Utah. We will see that this trend is only one of hundreds of global fault zones that formed between 1.6 and 1.7 billion years ago.

Some 16,000 feet of sedimentary rocks were deposited on top of this fractured basement in what was to become southwestern Colorado. Of course, it took more than 500 million years to accomplish this feat—from Cambrian time to the present. The resulting strata are exposed in continuous sequences in canyons near both Durango and Ouray on either flank of the dome. Such a clear record of geologic history is not known to occur any where else in the world. Although some chapters of this region's record book are missing, notably the Ordovician and Silurian systems, the rock column of Precambrian through Pleistocene times is laid bare in continuous sequence in these magnificent canyon walls. Even the heralded exposures of rock in Grand Canyon exhibit only strata of Precambrian through Paleozoic age; Mesozoic and Cenozoic rocks have been generally stripped from the canyon rims.

With such beautiful exposures of the rock record, geologists can identify the basement fault zone and date periods when fault movements occurred. We can see evidence of ancient shorelines that were positioned by topography created along the faults— how the seas came into this region and water depths varied because of fault movements, how great mountain chains rose along the faults, only to be eroded away, and how a deep, stagnant salt basin developed nearby. Further evidence shows that seas withdrew from the area for millions of years, only to return again in fairly recent geologic time, about 100 million years ago, and then departed again some 65 million years ago, never to return. The record of the rise of the San Juan dome and its early denudation is found in the San Juan Basin just south of Durango. Finally, deposits left by the melting glaciers form boulder-strewn ridges (moraines) in north Durango and other areas adjacent to the San Juan Mountains.

If we consider the San Juan dome to be a giant blister on the earth's crust at the juncture of the Colorado Plateau and southern Rocky Mountains, the entire geologic history of a key part of these provinces has been brought into view. We can see the complete history of the rise and fall of the ancestral Rocky Mountains and a second uplift of the ranges we know today. We can see sequences of rocks deposited in ancient seaways that lay hidden deep beneath the Colorado Plateau. In brief, we can see and study the secrets of two of the most beloved and spectacular geologic provinces in the great American West.

Chapter 2

It's About Time . . .

T he concept of geologic time is beyond human comprehension. We tend to think of time in terms of a few days, weeks, years, or decades, for these constitute a lifetime. A few hundred years is considered ancient history. It is impossible for us to conceive of a million years, a hundred million years, or (heaven help us!) a billion years. Yet the geologic history of the San Juan Mountains goes back more than 1.8 billion years!

Geologists are no different from everyone else regarding this matter, so they devised the Geologic Time Scale. With this scheme they could put chunks of time into handy boxes for easier reference and name the time boxes for pretty places where they enjoyed studying particular layers of rocks. Each box, a geologic time period, represented the time it took to deposit one's favorite bed of layered rocks—whatever length of time that might be.

Early attempts to establish a system of classifying spans of time were not very successful. For example, in 1766 Johann Gottlieb Lehmann proposed that mountain-building episodes be classified into (1) those that formed at the time of the creation of the earth, (2) those that formed during the time of the Flood, and (3) those that formed since the Flood. However, there have been hundreds of floods during the course of geologic time, so that scheme didn't work well.

By the 1830s, the scheme we now use began to emerge as a result of the work of a few British geologists, but not without some frustration. Adam Sedgwick studied and published descriptions of the oldest sedimentary rock sequence in the pleasant countryside in Wales, naming it the Cambrian System, Cambria being the Latin name for Wales. Almost simultaneously, Sir Roderick Murchison studied the sedimentary rocks along the border between England and Wales, naming his sequence the Silurian System, the Silures having been early inhabitants of the region. Both names were published in 1835. As luck would have it, some of the rocks included in each system were the same strata; the two systems overlapped. Predictably, a professional skirmish broke out. It continued until 1879, when Charles Lapworth settled the matter by naming the overlapping section the Ordovician System for another ancient tribe of people, the Ordovices. Murchison and Sedgwick, in 1839, had named the next younger geologic period the Devonian, for Devonshire, a lovely summer resort area in southwestern England.

The next younger sequence of rocks in the region is the Carboniferous System, the "coal measures" of central England. The actual coal-bearing beds are in the upper part, overlying a massive cliff-forming limestone known throughout western Europe as the Mountain Limestone. Although of totally different origin and surface appearance, the two rock types are still called the Lower Carboniferous and Upper Carboniferous in Europe. An almost identical sequence occurs in the eastern United States, where it was subdivided into the older (and therefore lower) Mississippian System and the younger Pennsylvanian System in 1869 and 1891, respectively. We use the two names effectively in this country, but European geologists still refuse to recognize the two American names in the Geologic Time Scale.

Sir Roderick Murchison was determined to name all rocks for a complete international Geologic Time Scale. He knew that an unnamed series of rocks existed between the Carboniferous

System of England and the much younger Triassic System of western Europe, but he was at a loss for an appropriate name. He obtained an invitation from Czar Nicholas I to visit Russia during the summers of 1840 and 1841 under the guise of determining if his other named systems of England and Wales were useful in eastern Europe. He traveled extensively in the Ural Mountains, where he found the missing section rather well exposed. In an 1841 report to the czar, he named the section of mostly red beds and evaporites the Permian System for the city of Perm and the extensive Perm Basin. Unfortunately, the section Murchison studied contains few distinctive fossils, and the lower boundary of the Permian System has never been accepted on an international basis.

At first, the absolute ages of rocks were an unknown, and the named boxes of geologic time were shuffled into order based on their relative position in the overall sequence of rocks. Thus, the oldest rocks were considered to be those at the bottom of the stack, as they must have already been in place before the next overlying layer could be deposited on top. This idea has become known as the Law of Superposition. In other words, rocks generally get older as you go deeper. Once the original order of the layered rocks was established, the contained fossils and their sequence of evolutionary changes have been utilized extensively to date and correlate sedimentary rocks on a global scale in a relative sense. During the ensuing 150 years, methods have been developed for measuring the age of rocks, in years, by studying radioactive decay rates.

The named geologic periods we have discussed are lumped into a larger unit, the Paleozoic Era (from the Greek *palaios*, meaning "old" and *zoe* meaning "life" or "ancient life"). Paleozoic time was preceded by the Precambrian Era, the first four billion years or so of earth history. No universally acceptable subdivision of the very lengthy Precambrian Era has ever been formally proposed despite numerous attempts. The Paleozoic Era was followed by the Mesozoic ("middle life") and that, in turn, by the Cenozoic ("late life").

The Mesozoic Era is subdivided into three geologic periods: the Triassic Period, named for a tripartite sequence of rocks in

Germany; the Jurassic Period, named for rocks of the Jura Alps along the French-Swiss border; and the Cretaceous Period, named for the chalk cliffs bordering the English Channel (from the Latin *creta* meaning "chalk").

The Cenozoic Era is subdivided into two periods, the names being carryovers from the first known geologic time scale, published in 1760 by Giovanni Arduina. He designated four periods, two of which were adapted into the present-day time scale: the Tertiary (third) Period and Quaternary (fourth) Period.

Rocks are Rocks are Rocks

There are three broad categories of rocks: igneous, metamorphic, and sedimentary. Each has a different story to tell.

Igneous rock forms as molten bodies cool and crystallize. If the molten mass cools beneath the earth's surface, it is called an *intrusive igneous rock;* a common example is granite. If hot liquids poured out at the surface from a volcano, either as lava or ash, an *extrusive igneous rock* results.

Metamorphic rock forms by the alteration of other rock types by intense heat and pressure deep within the earth. Minerals in the rock are distorted and/or new minerals are formed by partial melting and recrystallization. Resulting rock textures are mashed or wildly contorted and contain strange minerals such as mica or garnet. Metamorphic rocks are usually very old.

Sedimentary rocks contain compacted and/or cemented sediments, such as pebbles, sand, and mud, derived from the weathering of any other rock. Pebble deposits become conglomerate, sand is cemented to form sandstone, and mud compacts to shale. Limestone consists of calcium carbonate sediments, most of which are derived from the hard parts of marine plants and animals. They may occur as mud-size sediments or as sand- or pebble-size fragments of shell material, and fossils of complete shells are common. Most limestones were deposited in warm, shallow seas, where organic activity is high.

Rocks of all kinds are found in the San Juan Mountains. Igneous and metamorphic rocks, being more resistant to ero-

Table 1.
Geologic Time Scale

ERA	PERIOD	MILLIONS OF YEARS AGO	SAN JUAN MTNS FORMATIONS
CENOZOIC	Quaternary	0–1.6	Glacial Moraines Terrace gravel
	Tertiary	1.6–66.4	San Juan Volcanic S.J. Basin sediments McDermott Formation

MESOZOIC	Cretaceous	66.4–144	Kirtland/Fruitland
			Pictured Cliffs
			Lewis Shale
			Mesaverde Group
			    Cliffhouse Sandstone
			    Menefee Formation
			    Point Lookout Formation
			Mancos Shale
			Dakota Sandstone
			Burro Canyon Formation

	Jurassic	144–208	Morrison Formation Junction Cr. Sandstone Wanakah Formation Entrada Sandstone Wingate Sandstone?
	Triassic	208–245	Dolores Formation
PALEOZOIC	Permian	245–286	Cutler Formation

	Pennsylvanian	286–320	Hermosa Group:
			    Honaker Trail Formation
			    Paradox Formation
			    Pinkerton Trail
			      Formation
			Molas Formation

	Mississippian	320–360	Leadville Formation
	Devonian	360–408	Ouray Limestone Elbert Formation
	Silurian	408–438	rocks missing
	Ordovician	438–505	rocks missing
	Cambrian	505–570	Ignacio Formation
PRECAMBRIAN	Upper	570–2,500	Uncompahgre Quartzite Granite Twilight Gneiss
	Lower	2,500–4,500?	?

sion, occur in the highest peaks and ranges. Erosion has removed most of the sedimentary rock cover from the dome, exposing these harder, older rocks in the core. Erosional remnants of thick sedimentary rocks may be seen dipping away from the uplift in canyons carved from the flanks of the dome. A 16,000-foot-thick section of sedimentary rocks of Precambrian through Tertiary age has been exposed in the Animas Valley immediately north of Durango.

Keeping Track

Each layer of sedimentary rock has its own topographic expression, color, and mood. Any particular layer is different from those above and below, yet it can be traced laterally for miles or hundreds of miles across the country or through deep wells. Each layer of rock has a different geologic history and meaning; one is a stream deposit, another is an ancient field of windblown dunes, still another was deposited in shallow tropical seas. Because of this, it is important for geologists to distinguish among specific layers and to be able to communicate about any particular layer. So each is given a unique name, much like people have individual names.

Most people think of a rock *formation* as a silly-looking rock, perhaps shaped like an owl or an elephant. To a geologist, however, a rock formation is a layer, or series of similar layers, of rock that is geographically extensive, geologically significant, or both. Formation names are usually derived from a location, or *type section,* in which the layer(s) can best be studied. The name has two parts; the first part is a geographic place name, usually related to the type section, and the second part designates the kind of rock that typifies the formation.

For example, the gray slopes surrounding Durango are weathered from a very thick layer of marine gray shale named the Mancos Shale. The name "Mancos" comes from the type section along the Mancos River Valley that lies between Durango and Cortez, and the term *shale* explains the rock type. The overlying tan cliff, high to the west of town, is called the Point Lookout Sandstone, named for the prominent point at the entrance to Mesa Verde National Park and the fact that it consists of sandstone. The Mancos Shale extends into several states. It underlies the towns of Mancos, Cortez, and Grand Junction, besides Durango, and extends across the Rocky Mountains.

Sometimes a whole series of different, but closely related rock types occur in considerable thicknesses, making it impractical and unnecessary to name each bed. A series of interbedded red sandstones and shales occurs in the Animas Valley just north of Durango. Since the 2,500-foot-thick pile of red beds cannot properly be called either a sandstone or a shale, it is grouped as a formation, in this case, the Cutler Formation. The name "Cutler" comes from Cutler Creek just north of Ouray, where the same beds are well exposed; the name *Formation* means that it consists of more than one rock type.

Other times a formation may be given a name and later the rocks are found to be too complex and require subdividing into smaller units. In this case a formation can be elevated in rank to a *group* that can be divided into two or more formations. An example is the Hermosa Formation, named for rocks in Hermosa Mountain north of Durango, but later found to change elsewhere to different kinds of rocks. The formation was upgraded to the Hermosa Group, with three formations: the lower is the Pinkerton Trail Formation, the middle part is the Paradox Formation, and the upper, cliff-forming unit is called the Honaker Trail Formation. A formation may also be subdivided into *members*, which may or may not be given individual formal names. An example is the Elbert Formation, named for Elbert Creek near Purgatory Ski Area in the San Juan Mountains. In this case, the formation consists of a basal sandstone, named the McCracken Sandstone Member of the Elbert Formation, and an unnamed upper shale section. Notice how long and complex a member name can be.

All of this is designed to bring order out of chaos, and in most cases it usually works. Problems may arise when a single layer of rock is given different names in different areas. When this happens, the name first applied should be the one used. However, two names often result for the same rock layer. For example, limestone in the low, gray cliffs seen around Tamarron

Resort north of Durango is called the Leadville Limestone in Colorado, but it is the same bed that crops out in Grand Canyon, where it is called the Redwall Limestone. Since geologists at neither end will compromise, the same rock layer has two names.

The art of naming, correlating, studying, and keeping track of all this is called stratigraphy, and those who worry about it for a living are called stratigraphers.

Chapter 3

In the Beginning . . .

Not much is known about the birth of Planet Earth, except that it was a molten mass by about 4.5 billion years ago. Geophysicists speculate about how this hot blob came into existence, but it matters little, as rocks of this age have never been found on earth, and probably never will be. The oldest earth rocks to date have been thought to be African, dating at about 3.6 billion years, but in 1989, rocks dating at 3.96 billion years were found in the Slave Province of northern Canada. Rocks on the moon are about 4.2 billion years old.

Dating of such ancient rocks is accomplished by careful study of radioactive minerals. A radioactive element, such as uranium, decays through time by losing nuclear particles of helium. A new element, called the daughter element, is formed in place of the original (parent) material. In the case of uranium, the daughter is a peculiar variety of lead (there are several kinds of uranium, with varying breeds of lead). If the decay rate can be determined and the amount of remaining parent and daughter elements can be measured, the time when the original mineral formed can be estimated. Because radioactive decay rates are approximate, the results are not as accurate as one might wish, but such measurements in hundreds of millions of years are remarkably good. To complicate matters, the "rock clock" is reset each time the mineral gets hot enough to be recrystallized. Such ancient rocks may have been "refried" several times.

The Basement

The oldest rocks exposed in the San Juan Mountains date at a little less than two billion years, or about middle Precambrian, so the record of more than half of earth's history is not documented here. Even at that, the rocks are so gnarled, twisted, and mashed that it is uncertain what kinds of rocks they were before the process of metamorphism began. Such metamorphic rocks- those that have been highly altered by heat and high pressures— are called *schists* and *gneisses* (pronounced "shist" and "nice"). Geologists give formal names to such bodies of rock to distinguish one from another. These oldest Precambrian rocks in the high San Juan Mountains are called the Twilight Gneiss for exposures in Twilight Peak, the highest mountain in the West Needles Range north of Durango. They can be seen along the old road in the deep canyon of Lime Creek, in the vicinity of Coal Bank Pass, and in the upper Animas River canyon south of Silverton. Rocks of similar age and appearance in Grand Canyon are called the Vishnu Schist.

Rocks of the Twilight Gneiss must have undergone intense kneading at great depths beneath the surface of the earth, where temperatures are sufficiently extreme to cause partial melting and severe distortion of preexisting rocks and minerals. This thoroughly stirred "mess" was then somehow brought up to the surface and exposed to weathering processes. Erosion leveled the land to a near plane before the next geologic event. How all this actually occurred is anybody's guess, as this stage of geologic history is truly lost in antiquity.

What we need to understand at this point is that when the Twilight Gneiss was formed and exposed at the earth's surface, the land was nothing at all as we see it today. There were no mountains, at least in their present form. None of the thousands of feet of layered rocks that now cover the Precambrian basement had been formed. There were no trees, no grass, no

The West Needle Mountains from north of Coal Bank Pass. The high mountains are in the older Precambrian Twilight Gneiss, but the inclined ridges in the middle distance are nearly vertical beds of Uncompahgre Quartzite, faulted against the metamorphic complex about halfway up the mountainside.

animals—indeed the only life on earth was the simplest forms of single-celled plants, called algae, and bacteria. Thus, the lands, the entire continent, and all continents, were barren rock. The scene would have made the Sahara Desert appear lush by comparison. There may have been little or no oxygen in the air, as that is believed to have formed from plant photosynthesis, and life was still in its most primitive stage of development as unicellular and simple filamentous algae and bacteria. Yet this monotonous, barren wasteland would form the basis for all future geologic events. The Twilight Gneiss would serve as the foundation in southwest Colorado upon which all later rocks would be deposited, the rocks into which all later molten masses would intrude, the surface that all future fractures would break and faults would dislocate, the rock that would disintegrate by

In the Beginning . . .

weathering to form sediments. This was the known beginning of geologic time in what would become southwestern Colorado, the basement upon which all geological architecture would be built.

Whose Fault Is It?

If there is a rock to break, it will be broken! Cracks in rocks are called fractures, or joints, and if there is movement of any kind along the fracture it is called a *fault*. The Twilight Gneiss now formed in this corner of the continent was destined to be faulted!

There are several kinds of faults, depending upon the direction of movement that occurs along the fracture. The kind of movement is dependent on the forces acting upon the earth's crust—where they are coming from and going to.

There are *normal faults,* but no abnormal faults. A normal fault occurs where one side of the fracture drops down relative to the other side. Surprisingly, the side that drops down is called the down-thrown block and the high side is called the up-thrown block. Normal faults form where the earth's crust is being pulled apart by extensional forces. If a block of rock is downdropped between two normal faults it is called a *graben* (German for a "ditch" or "grave"). If a block of rock is left high, stranded between two grabens, it is called a *horst* (another German word, but with no direct English equivalent). Normal faults actually lengthen the crust and are consequently also known as *extensional faults.*

There are *reverse faults,* but no forward faults. Reverse faults occur when rocks above the fault (hanging wall) are pushed upward over the lower side (foot wall) at a relative high angle. If movement occurs at a low angle it is called a *thrust fault.* These faults form where the crust of the earth is crowded or jammed by compressional forces. Usually, layered rocks will first fold into sharp kinks and later break as horizontal compression exceeds the strength of the rocks, forming a thrust or reverse fault. These faults shorten the earth's crust.

Wrench faults are the worst kind. They are faults along which movement is mostly lateral, rather than vertical. One side moves to the right or left of the opposite side, although up or down may occur on a lessor scale. Usually wrench faults occur as swarms or zones of faulting, rather than as single faults. These faults do everything wrong and may appear to be normal, reverse, or even thrust faults; some do all these things some-where along their trace. They can "yo-yo" (first one side is up, then the other), they can "scissor" (change from a normal to a reverse fault at a hinge point), or they can do "(c) all of the above" and more. Once wrench faulting is initiated, it usually recurs episodically throughout the rest of geologic history. In other words, if the faults are sort of crazy and don't fit a reasonable pattern or history, they are probably wrench faults.

The many faults that cause numerous earthquakes in southern California are wrench faults; the San Andreas fault is the most famous. In that case, the seaward (western) block is moving northward relative to the landward (eastern) block. If one stands on one side and looks across at the other side of the fault, the opposite side is moving to the right, regardless of which angle is taken. Because of this the sense of relative movement along the San Andreas fault is said to be right-lateral. There are many crooked fence lines in southern California, having been offset to the right by a fault. The San Andreas and other California right-lateral wrench faults trend to the northnorthwest. However, some faults in the area, such as the Garlock fault, trend easterly and display a left-lateral sense of relative movement. So how can that happen?

It has been proven experimentally that if a block of solid rock is placed in a vise and the vise is tightened in a north-south direction, the rock will fracture and fault along predictable trends. X-shaped faults trending northwest and northeast will break across the rock simultaneously. The northwesterly faults will invariably be right-lateral and the northeast faults left-lateral. So compressional forces acting from north to south will cause the observed relationships in California. However, in this case the continent is thought to be overriding the oceanic sea floor at an oblique angle, causing oblique strain which results in a similar fault pattern.

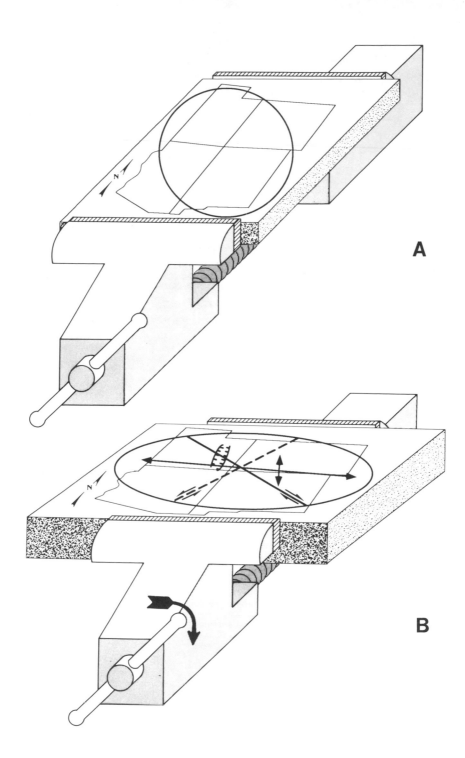

A

B

The Bigger Picture

It so happens that the basement of Twilight Gneiss now exposed in the San Juan Mountains was torn asunder by wrench faults that appear to be nearly identical to the California fault system. The overall trend is the same, the right-lateral sense of displacement is the same, and it is believed that faults of the San Juan Mountains bordered the continent in Precambrian time. The main difference is that these faults were bringing about their earthquakes some 1.7–1.6 billion years ago, instead of last week. Fortunately, no buildings were around to be collapsed.

We now realize that the exposed faults in the crest of the San Juan Mountains are a small segment of a continental-scale fault zone. In fact, this and a small area in north-central New Mexico

Fig. 1. The crust of the earth is brittle, from a geologic perspective, and will break along predictable trends when subjected to compression. A block of the crust covering an area the size of Utah, Colorado, New Mexico, and Arizona—as in **A**—can be used to show the effects of compression. An imaginary giant circle around the area, tightened vise-like, will create compressional stress in a north-south direction. The block will first break along northeast and northwest fractures. If the application of compression continues, movement will occur along the fracture zones, and wrench faulting (lateral rather than vertical movement) begins. Notice that the circle has turned into an elongate spheroid, and the outline of the states has been shortened from north to south and broadened from east to west. Wrench faulting must occur to accommodate the crustal shortening in one direction and extension in the other. Faults trending to the northwest will invariably be right lateral, and northeast-trending faults will move in a left-lateral sense (see the small arrows in **B**). Secondary structures consist of folds and/or thrust faults that trend east-west, normal to the compressional stress field, and extensional faults (normal faults) occur in north-south trends that are normal to the direction of least compression (or extension). Precambrian basement faults in the San Juan Mountains and the neighboring Colorado Plateau probably formed in this manner, although torsional stress on the block would have had the same effect.

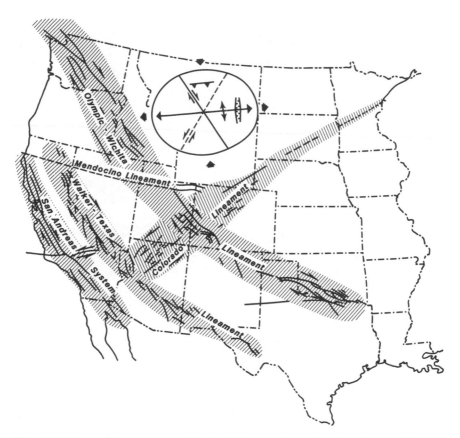

Fig. 2. Map of the western United States showing locations of significant basement wrench fault zones that affect the San Juan Mountain region. Note the kink in southwest Colorado, the Grenadier and Sneffels fault blocks, where the northwesterly fault zone is slightly offset by the northeasterly fault zone; both fault trends date at about 1.7 billion years. The Walker Lane-Texas lineament to the southwest parallels the Olympic-Wichita, but is slightly younger, with initial movements dated at about 1.3 billion years. The San Andreas wrench fault system in California is still in motion today, but is otherwise similar to the Precambrian counterparts. Sense of lateral movements on the fault zones are shown by small arrows.

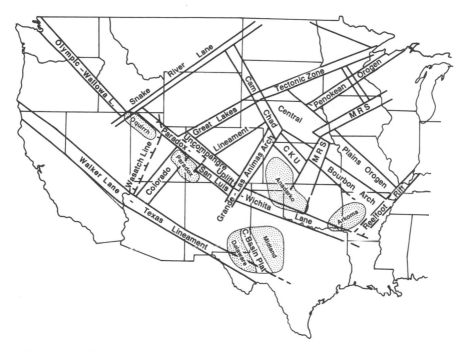

Fig. 3. Regional map of the western United States showing locations and trends of known major basement wrench fault belts. Also illustrated are the close relationships of some important sedimentary basins of late Paleozoic age (stippled areas). This shows what occurs when a larger vise acts upon a larger continental block.

are the only known exposures of the faults. All other evidence of the existence of the megarift is from geophysical studies and deep wells. The major trend of wrench faulting extends from Oklahoma through southwestern Colorado and across Utah. It may extend to the northwest as far as offshore British Columbia, but that has been called an outrageous hypothesis. A number of northwest- and northeast-trending fault zones similar to this one extend across North America. Indeed, they occur on every continent and are all about the same age.

New Old Rocks

If huge blocks of the continent are sliding past one another, they must be coming from someplace and going someplace.

But where? The rock that is faulted against the Twilight Gneiss is of a completely different nature. It does not seem to have been deposited here on the Twilight Gneiss, because it is about the same age as the Twilight Gneiss, yet it is not nearly so highly metamorphosed. What seems to be at the bottom of the stack is a thick conglomerate called the Vallecito Conglomerate, overlain by the Irving Greenstone, a much-smashed pile of old sedimentary and volcanic rocks, tentatively dated at 1.78 billion years. The qualification on its position in the sequence results from the complex faulting and limited exposures found only in the canyons of the Pine and Vallecito rivers.

It would also appear that the Irving is overlain by conglomerates called the Middle Mountain Conglomerate and in turn by a very thick pile of quartzite called the Uncompahgre Formation. Quartzite is simply a metamorphic form of very hard sandstone, and the formation includes some slate, or highly squeezed shale. Thickness of this ancient sand pile has been estimated to be greater than 10,000 feet. However, its base is not exposed and there is no known top to the formation. Yes, there was a top and bottom to the deposits originally, but we just can't find them in this faulted madhouse in the San Juan Mountains. These rocks form the obviously upturned and highly faulted layered rocks in the Grenadier Range south of Silverton and in Uncompahgre Canyon, from which it was named, immediately south of Ouray.

At first it seemed as though this new section of rocks had been deposited on the Twilight Gneiss and later dropped down adjacent to the Twilight by normal faults. As evidence accumulated that these are wrench faults, however, that interpretation became obsolete, and if the age of the Irving Greenstone is anywhere near correct, it would be impossible. So where did all this mountain of different rock come from? A very similar sequence of ancient quartzite occurs in northern New Mexico, but it lies along the same wrench fault zone. It is probable that the rock was all rifted into place from some distant area, such as Oklahoma or Idaho. It would be a great help to know the age of the quartzites, but no fossils were preserved in these rocks and they contain no radioactive minerals. The great sand pile could be older than the Twilight Gneiss, the same age, or younger.

Whatever the true answers may be, the fault zone is definitely present, and will come back to haunt us throughout the remainder of geologic time. And remember that the fault zone is traceable for hundreds of miles, both toward the southeast into Oklahoma and northwestward, at least across Utah.

Hot Rocks

After faulting was well underway and the quartzite section was in place, a period of intrusive igneous activity occurred in what would become the San Juan Mountains. The word *igneous* refers to fire, and in geologic circles it means that there was sufficient heat available to melt rocks in the earth's crust. If the resulting molten mass tried to elbow its way to the surface and didn't make it, the cooled rocks are called *intrusive igneous rocks*. If they reached the surface, they flowed as lavas or ash that cooled to form *extrusive igneous rocks*. In this case, they did not reach the surface and cooled to become several bodies of granite. Because granitic rocks contain radioactive minerals, they can be dated. In the San Juan Mountains the time of cooling of various granite bodies is used to date early fault movements.

Here's how it works. Our old friend, the Twilight Gneiss was dated at 1.76 billion years plus or minus 20 million years. "Plus or minus 20 million years" may sound like a lot of time, but it is only a lunch break considering that Precambrian time was four billion years of earth history. The Twilight Gneiss is cut by the faults, so it had to be there when faulting occurred. So faulting occurred not before but after minerals crystallized in the metamorphic terrain some 1.76 billion years ago. One of the granite bodies, known as the Ten Mile Granite, was dated at 1.72 billion years old. It was cut by one of the faults near Elk Park in the Animas River canyon south of Silverton, so fault movement must have occurred not before but after that date as well. One of the largest granitic bodies in the San Juan Mountains, the Eolus (pronounced "ay-oh!-less") Granite, named for Eolus Peak in the Needle Range, intruded and gobbled up both the Twilight Gneiss and the Uncompahgre Quartzite that are separated by the faults. Thus, the faults were present prior to emplacement of the Eolus Granite, and it has been dated at 1.46 billion years. So our faults must have moved sometime between 1.46 and 1.72 billion years ago. Worldwide, an episode of continental-scale wrench faulting began about 1.7 billion years ago and culminated at about 1.6 billion years ago. Our timing on these faults fits that global pattern beautifully, so we could guess that much of the early fault movement in what are now the high San Juan Mountains occurred 1.6–1.7 billion years ago.

Where to Look

A quick look at the simplified geologic map of the San Juan Mountains (Fig. 4) shows us where to look for the rocks and faults we are talking about. The main faults are the heavy lines that trend east-west across the area at Coal Bank Pass and at Molas Lake. Outcrops of Twilight Gneiss occur south of the Coal Bank fault and north of the Molas Lake-Beartown fault in and near the Animas River canyon and in the West Needles Mountains.

Along each of the two large faults at Coal Bank Pass and Molas Lake, the Uncompahgre quartzite and slate sequence is faulted against the Twilight. Thus, the large block of quartzite lies in a Precambrian graben (down-faulted block). The quartzite terrain is also highly folded and faulted within the graben, and is seen in the Grenadier Range across the canyon from Molas Lake and in Snowdon Peak above Molas Pass. Uncompahgre Creek, south of Ouray along the Million Dollar Highway, has carved a magnificent canyon into near-vertical beds of Uncompahgre quartzite. Eolus Granite forms the Needle Mountains, best viewed to the east from U.S. Highway 550 a few miles south of Purgatory Ski Area.

The more generalized regional map portrays the geographic extent of the exposed fault system and the individual fault blocks. The southern block of quartzite has been called the Grenadier fault block, named for the Grenadier Range in which

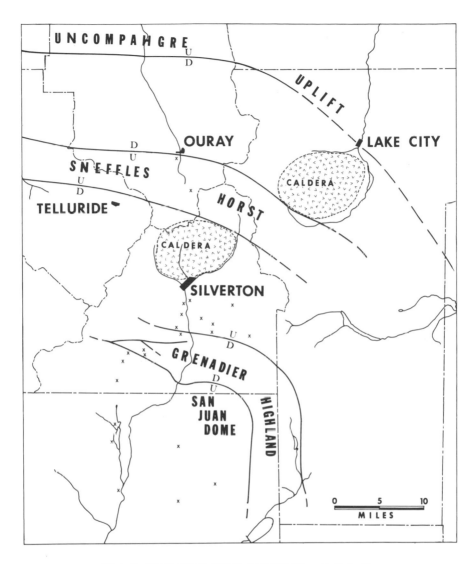

PALEOTECTONIC MAP

SAN JUAN MOUNTAINS

Fig. 4. Map of the San Juan Mountain region showing the Grenadier and Sneffels basement fault blocks. The patterned areas are volcanic vents of Tertiary age that occur between the basement fault blocks. Detailed studies were conducted at the sites marked by small Xs.

The Sneffels Range viewed from the south, near Telluride, which lies in the intervening valley. The lower foothills are in the Cutler Formation (Permian). The higher mountains were eroded from rocks of the San Juan Volcanic series of Tertiary age.

it is found, and the northern one is called the Sneffels block for exposures in and near the Sneffels Range west of Ouray. Both fault blocks extend for hundreds of miles, both to the southeast toward Oklahoma and to the northwest into Utah. On the map the regional trend of faulting is obviously northwest-southeast, but in the San Juan Mountains a large westerly "kink" has developed. It appears that the regional pattern has been offset and dragged westerly by the House Creek and Hogback faults, two northeast-oriented left-lateral wrench faults. When the San Juan dome was formed much later, about 65 million years ago, the kink and its included massive body of Eolus Granite served

Angular unconformity at the high bridge atop Box Canyon near Ouray. The near-vertical quartzite below is in the Precambrian Uncompahgre Formation, which was upturned and then bevelled by erosion before the nearly horizontal thin-bedded dolomites of the upper Elbert Formation were deposited in late Devonian time. Typical of both the Grenadier and here in the Sneffels fault blocks, the quartzite was topographically high during deposition of the Cambrian Ignacio and Devonian McCracken Sandstone Member of the Elbert Formation, as those units are missing. The upper cliff is in the Ouray and Leadville formations.

In the Beginning . . .

Huge ripple marks, an estimated three feet from crest-to-crest, on a nearvertical bedding plane of the Precambrian Uncompahgre Quartzite. View is across Uncompahgre Creek at Bear Creek Falls overlook south of Ouray. These must have been formed in strong currents of relatively deep water.

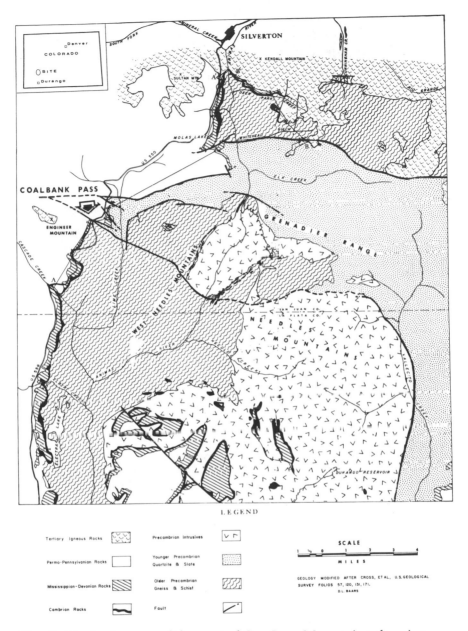

Fig. 5. Geologic map of the central San Juan Mountains showing the geographic distribution of rock exposures, by ages. The map has been slightly modified from the folio maps published by Cross and his associates in the late 1890s.

In the Beginning . . .   33 as a sort of knot in the earth's crust, causing the uplift to be ovate rather than elongate like other structures in the region.

The rock record of much of Precambrian time is missing here following the intrusion of the Eolus Granite about 1.46 billion years ago. Remember that the molten granite did not reach the surface, but cooled underground. Some kind of rock must have been present above the intrusive body, but it was removed by erosion before Paleozoic sedimentary rocks were deposited about 500 million years ago. In short, more than a billion years of late Precambrian time is unaccounted for. Whatever happened, a ridge and valley, rather gentle topography, was preserved at the surface as late Cambrian seas inundated the terrain 500 million years ago. The quartzite blocks formed low ridges, islands, or promontories, and the gneiss and granite outcrops were valleys, or shallow inlets of the sea, as sands that would become the Ignacio Quartzite were spread across the land in Cambrian time.

Where did all that sediment go that was removed from the Precambrian basement during the billion years before Cambrian time? That is anybody's guess. Thick sedimentary deposits of this age are found to the west in Grand Canyon and to the north in the Uinta Mountains. Perhaps the exposed basement of the San Juan Mountains contributed to these deposits. The story would make a good mystery novel.

Chapter 4

The Early Years

The present-day Rocky Mountain and Colorado Plateau regions were well above sea level at the beginning of Cambrian time, 570 million years ago. Sea level was on the rise, however, and the shoreline began a painstakingly slow journey eastward from Nevada across the continental margin and shelf. Erosion had nearly leveled the Precambrian landscape, but here and there, as in present-day Grand Canyon and the San Juan Mountains, hills of quartzite rose above the land. As the shoreline passed these low hills, they formed islands for a time, but in Grand Canyon country they were gradually buried by coastal sands of the Cambrian sea. It took 70 million years, or until latest Cambrian time, for the beaches to reach the present site of the San Juan Mountains.

Early Cambrian time was also when the first marine animals with preservable hard parts (shells) evolved. Shells of trilobites (small marine crab-like critters) and brachiopods (shelled life something like clams) dominated marine animal life. Some of their remains became fossils in the sandstones and shales that were deposited. Because these animals evolved rather rapidly, at least in geologic time spans, they are useful in dating the rocks. Not a single trilobite has been found in Cambrian rocks, called

Quartzite boulder conglomerate in the Ignacio Formation along the Snowdon fault near Lime Creek.

the Ignacio Formation, in the San Juan Mountains, but they were lurking somewhere nearby. Their tracks, trails, and resting places are preserved on sandstone bedding planes at several localities.

Whitman Cross, a U.S. Geological Survey geologist who first mapped the geology of the San Juan Mountains in the 1890s, found one complete and one broken brachiopod in the Ignacio Formation. Experts at the time believed that the small, primitive shells were of Cambrian age. It was not until the mid1950s that a few other specimens were discovered, and in about 1960, we found thousands of the little critters on a single bedding plane in Cascade Creek north of Purgatory Ski Area. The fossils are oval-shaped, usually black phosphatic shells with circular growth lines. The bivalved animals had no hinges, only muscles to hold the two shells in place, so the fossils occur as single shells laid open-side down on the bedding surface. Because one cannot see the inside of the shells, they can be identified only as genus *Obolus*; the species name cannot be determined. The time range of *Obolus* is latest Cambrian to earliest Ordovician, and the Ignacio Formation is believed to be very late Cambrian in age.

The Precambrian fault blocks of quartzite stood as islands and peninsulas along the shoreline of the Cambrian sea as it encroached upon present-day southwestern Colorado. Boulders on talus-covered slopes that formed the shoreline were incorporated into the beach sands and remain as conglomerates at edges of both the Coal Bank and Molas faults. These are only narrow bands of conglomerate, however, and the Ignacio changes to sandstone and in turn to shale at very short distances away from the faults. Here one can walk along the beds and see shoreline boulders of quartzite nearly two feet in diameter change to beach and offshore sandstone in 100 or 200 feet of exposure, and to offshore, quiet water shale in less than a mile. In brief, boulders at the shoreline changed over short distances to nearshore sands and then to deeper-water muds between the Precambrian fault blocks. The islands were never buried by sediments in Cambrian time.

So the quartzite fault blocks were high and above sea level in latest Cambrian time, as shown on the generalized cross-sections (Fig. 6). They were being down-faulted in Precambrian time when we saw them last; sense of movement on the faults had reversed, but remember that yo-yo movements along wrench faults are to be expected.

By the close of Cambrian time, sea level began to fall relative to the lands. The sea gradually shrank back from present-day western Utah and Nevada, returning to where it had come from, not to rise and inundate the land again for nearly three geologic periods. No rocks of Ordovician or Silurian age have been found in the San Juan Mountains nor across the Colorado Plateau country toward the western seaway. The vast lowland seemed to lie dormant until late in the Devonian Period a hundred million years later in geologic history.

Such a break in the rock record, where there are no deposits to represent known geologic time, is called an *unconformity*. It is thought that some layers were deposited but eroded before the

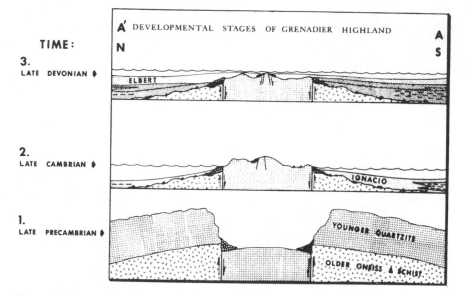

Fig. 6. Generalized cross-sections showing developmental stages of the Grenadier fault block. Stage 1, the oldest, is the most hypothetical, as the younger Precambrian quartzites and slates may have been emplaced by wrench faulting rather than by vertical fault juxtaposition as shown.

next (late Devonian in this case) preserved sediments blanketed the Cambrian surface, creating another great unsolved mystery.

The Devonian

When the sea finally made its way back to the present Rocky Mountain region and southwestern Colorado, it was already late Devonian time. Nearly three geologic periods of time had elapsed, leaving no record in the rocks whatsoever.

Sandy beaches formed in southwestern Colorado and a few offshore bars built up along high fault blocks in present-day east-central Utah in late Devonian time. The resulting sandstone is called the McCracken Sandstone Member of the Elbert Formation. Elsewhere across the Colorado Plateau region to the west, only bleak, limy tidal flats resulted. As late Devonian time progressed, lime-mud tidal flats covered the sand deposits, and

Lower Paleozoic section near Rockwood Quarry. The Cambrian Ignacio Formation is covered by talus, lower right; the lower cliff is the McCracken Sandstone Member grading up into the tree-covered slope of the upper member of the Elbert Formation, both of late Devonian age. The Ouray Limestone is below the prominent notch at the base of the upper cliff, and the thin-bedded dolomite above the notch is the lower member of the Mississippian Leadville Formation. The massive cliff at the top is the upper Leadville.

the unnamed upper member of the Elbert Formation was deposited across the entire region.

Sand of the McCracken Member lapped up against the quartzite fault blocks in the present-day San Juan Mountains, but did not bury them. Either the quartzite hills were again uplifted along the faults, or they may have simply remained high since Cambrian time. The hills must have been relatively low by this time, as shoreline conglomerate has only been found at one small locality high on the west flank of Snowdon Peak at the north-bounding fault of the Grenadier block. The upper Elbert tidal flats buried most of the remaining topography.

Tidal flats that extended for hundreds of miles onto the North American continent were common in lower Paleozoic time. In the case of the Elbert Formation, intertidal mud flats apparently extended all the way to the open sea that lay at least 200 miles to the west. Several sedimentary features typify tidal-flat deposits. Preserved mud cracks, small ripple marks, raindrop impressions, worm burrows, and thin, crinkly beds called stromatolites formed on algal-coated bedding surfaces help identify these deposits. In a very arid climate, gypsum or salt crystals may form just beneath the sediment surface; cube-shaped salt casts are common in the Elbert Formation.

Another characteristic of lime-mud tidal flats is that the original calcium-carbonate sediment is rapidly converted to dolomite. The process involves adding magnesium molecules to the calcium-carbonate crystal structure and is called dolomitization. This is easily accomplished on higher levels of tidal flats. The sediments are soaked and ponds formed during very high tides, leaving the seawater to evaporate and concentrate the salts during low tide. As magnesium becomes highly concentrated, it reacts very quickly with lime sediments to form the new crystal structure. The Elbert Formation is a thinly bedded dolomite containing all sedimentary structures that characterize tidal-flat deposits.

Because the upper Elbert Formation is thin-bedded and shaly, it weathers to form gentle tree- and soil-covered slopes. The only places where the rocks are exposed are roadcuts and rare areas along steep stream channels. The best place to view the formation is the long roadcut between Cascade Creek and Coal Bank Pass, south of the pass.

Sea level continued its gradual rise until after the end of Devonian time. When it reached a point where the tidal flats were completely under water, shaly dolomites of the Elbert Formation were gradually buried and overlain by shallow marine lime mud. Although the change in rock type is very gradual, the overlying dark, usually brown, massive, dense limestone is distinctive. It was named the Ouray Limestone for the massive limestone cliffs south of Ouray, but the upper part of those cliffs has since been renamed the Leadville Limestone.

The Ouray Limestone was deposited so near the Devonian-Mississippian time boundary that its fossils didn't really know

The square-shaped objects on this bedding surface of upper Elbert dolomite are salt casts formed on a late Devonian tidal mud flat. These specimens are from highway roadcuts between Cascade Creek and Coal Bank Pass along U.S. Highway 550.

in which geologic period they lived. Brachiopods, the clam-like bivalves, thought it was still late Devonian time; Foraminifera, tiny one-celled marine animals, were more optimistic and believed that it was already Mississippian time. Some paleontologists (people who study fossils) like to believe in the conodonts, microscopic tooth-like structures used by a long-extinct variety of worms, who agreed with the brachiopods in self-defense. Since we really don't know whom to believe, it seems likely that the formation was deposited even as the calendar was changing. The lower Ouray Limestone is probably latest Devonian in age and the top may be early Mississippian. Some geologists place the formation in the Devonian for convenience.

Meanwhile, the major wrench faults were not completely dormant. Islands and peninsulas of Precambrian quartzite re-

Lower Paleozoic section above Box Canyon near Ouray. The lower, ledgy slope is the upper member of the Elbert Formation, and the upper cliff is the combined Ouray and Leadville formations. Sandstone cliffs in the Pennsylvanian Hermosa Group may be seen in the shaded, upper area.

mained high, or were again elevated along the faults, as the Elbert Formation was deposited. The McCracken Sandstone (lower) Member abuts the Coal Bank Pass fault, but does not cross over the fault. In the Molas Lake area, the McCracken thins and pinches out one-half mile north of the Molas-Beartown fault. Upper Elbert shaly dolomites were deposited across the faults, however, and rest directly on upturned Precambrian quartzite layers across the high fault blocks, burying the ancient topography for the first time. Another of these angular uncon-formities is beautifully exposed at the high bridge above Box Canyon at Ouray.

Then it happened again: by the time Ouray Limestone beds blanketed the Elbert mudflats, the faults were reversing their movement. High on the flanks of the Grenadier fault block, marine muds of the Ouray change to tidal flat dolomites, meaning that seawater shallowed to intertidal conditions toward the faults. That is what would be expected; however, exposures of Ouray Limestone on the quartzite block across the faults contain fossils of open marine animals, therefore what had been higher land suddenly was inundated by marine waters.

Crinoids Inherit the Earth

As the geological calendar was turning over from Devonian to Mississippian time, sea level dropped once again. Extensive tidal flats covered with lime mud formed from the present-day Rocky Mountains westward into Nevada. Resulting thin-bedded dolomites covered the entire region, attaining thicknesses varying from only a few feet to a couple of hundred feet. We call these beds the lower member of the Leadville Formation in Colorado; they constitute the lower two members of the Redwall Limestone in the Grand Canyon. The entire region was briefly exposed to erosion, forming a minor unconformity. This ancient land surface was very flat, however, and it is difficult to see in the rocks.

When the sea returned to the present-day Colorado Plateau and Rocky Mountains provinces, thick lime mud was deposited that would become the massive limestone cliffs everywhere it is exposed today. These deposits are seen in Grand Canyon as the high, prominent cliffs of the upper Redwall Limestone and the massive, gray cliffs in the vicinity of Tamarron Resort north of Durango. Here, it is known as the upper member of the Leadville Formation. Wherever the sea floor was raised to near sea level, especially on the flanks of the high fault blocks, shoals consisting of crinoid debris formed.

Crinoids may look like plants, but they are really animals of the phylum Echinodermata. In those days, they lived attached to the sea floor by holdfast systems that resemble roots, stood above the bottom on long, skinny stalks that resemble stems, and had flower-like heads and petal-like arms. They fed on passing microscopic plants and animals. It is no wonder that

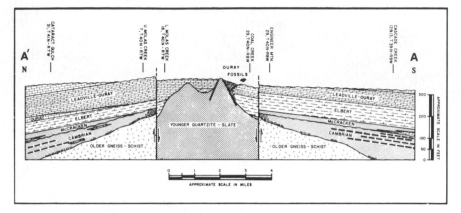

Fig. 7. Generalized cross-section showing the stratigraphic changes in the various formations in the vicinity of the Grenadier fault block at the end of Mississippian time. This diagram is a continuation, with regard to time, of the cross-sections shown in Fig. 6.

living descendants are called "sea lilies" today, although most are now unattached and float about in relatively deep waters. Hard structures made of calcite strengthened the animals. These consisted of button-shaped segments that were closely fit, but flexible, in all segments except the heads, which were built of interlocking plates. Crinoid heads are extremely rare as fossils; perhaps primitive fish grazed on the heads and destroyed the cup-shaped structures. When the animals died, the segments fell apart to form lime sand grains that often piled up into sizable banks, or mounds, on the sea floor. For some unknown reason, crinoids proliferated in Mississippian time throughout the global seas. Fossil crinoid parts are abundant in all limestones of this age and may be the entire rock-forming constituent. Truly, crinoids came to dominate life in the sea.

The best exposures of crinoidal limestones in the upper Leadville Formation are between Shalona Lake and Coal Bank Pass north of Durango, the white rock hummocks around Molas Lake, and above Box Canyon at Ouray. At all of these locations, the rock is very pure calcium carbonate and therefore white in color, and it consists of nearly 100 percent crinoid fossils. The large lens-shaped limestone cliff immediately south of Box

Molas Lake Campground at the top of the Mississippian Leadville Formation. The high country of the Grenadier Range consists of strongly thrust-faulted Precambrian quartzite.

Canyon at Ouray is a crinoid bank. The knobs and hummocks of limestone near Molas Lake are karst towers, remnants from intense underground drainage and deep weathering, eroded from another crinoid bank.

Several of these crinoid banks exist deep underground in southwestern Colorado and east-central Utah. They are identical to banks seen in the San Juan Mountains, but some have been altered to dolomite and have become excellent reservoirs for oil and gas.

Ancient Soil

By middle Mississippian time, the sea had again withdrawn westward from the shallow marine shelf environments of Colorado and eastern Utah to the open, deep sea that flowed across western Utah and Nevada. Limestones of the Leadville-Redwall formations lay exposed to weathering on a vast, low plain for the last half of Mississippian time and during the early years of the Pennsylvanian Period. The climate was hot and humid, and a thick, red soil, called laterite, formed on the plains. Because the rocks at the surface were limestone, underground drainage developed easily, with caves and sinkholes forming an extensive drainage network. This so-called karst surface is exposed at the top of the Leadville Formation in the San Juan Mountains in the form of a few fossil sinkholes and caves, such as in Rockwood quarry north of Durango, and remnant karst towers at Molas Lake (properly pronounced "mole!-us").

The ancient red soil, called the Molas Formation, can be seen in roadcuts near Purgatory Ski Area and around Molas Lake, from which the name was derived. It is present everywhere at the top of the Leadville Formation, but because it is soft and weathers to low slopes on Leadville benches, it is usually covered with talus and modern soil. The age of the Molas Formation is not well known, but it must have begun forming in late Mississippian time when the Leadville was exposed to weathering. Early Pennsylvanian fossils occur in the upper red shale near Molas Lake, but they were deposited as Pennsylvanian seas again invaded the region.

Until this point in geologic history, the region we call the Colorado Plateau and southern Rockies was covered repeatedly by shallow seas. Only minor recurrent movements of the wrench faults disturbed the sea floor. The shallow seas were vast, covering the present-day mountain region from Mexico to Alaska with shallow-water marine deposits, mostly limestones and dolomites. But things would be different during the next geologic period.

Ancestral Rockies

W hat happened to the world shortly after the beginning of Pennsylvanian time was not a pretty sight. Mountain chains popped up on all the continents; deep, faulted basins sagged into existence; ice caps formed in the polar regions; and sea level bounced around, first rising to inundate continents, only to fall again leaving dead fish everywhere. If you had been a clam in Europe or Asia, you would have called this the Hercynian orogeny, in North America the ancestral Rocky Mountains orogeny. *Orogeny* is the term geologists use for an episode of mountain building. Despite the extreme changes in global structure that occurred at this time in geologic history, European geologists still do not accept the American term "Pennsylvanian Period," but call it the Upper Carboniferous Period.

The plate tectonics concept concludes that each continent and vast parts of ocean floors act as individual plates of the earth's crust that migrate across the globe, perhaps colliding with one another and then sometimes diving to the depths of the earth to be recycled. The rock reemerges at the surface in the form of volcanic material along the mid-oceanic ridges. As continental plates collide, mountain ranges and intervening basins form. Such events occurred several times before the continents assumed their present-day configurations. One such event must have been during the early days of the Pennsylvanian Period. Even then, the activity took place along fault systems already in existence across the globe since Precambrian time.

In addition to unruly structural developments on a global scale, fluctuating sea levels marred the geologic records of the Pennsylvanian Period. Repeatedly rising and falling sea levels have in the past been rather lightly explained. Abundant evidence shows that extensive glaciers capped the polar regions during Pennsylvanian and early Permian times. When vast, continental-scale glaciers develop, the water they trap comes from the sea, and sea level falls. As glaciers melt, water is released back to the sea and sea level rises. A waterbudget problem such as this occurred at least four times within the past million years or so, during the great Ice Age. More than 100 such cycles of glaciation and sea level fluctuation occurred during the late Paleozoic, affecting sedimentation patterns on all of the continents.

Ancestral Rocky Mountains

We have seen that our wrench fault zone extends from Oklahoma northwestward into Utah, and perhaps beyond. These faults were strongly reactivated early in Pennsylvanian time. Great mountain ranges formed by uplift along the east side of each major fault zone, and deep, elongate basins sagged between the uplifts. The momentous occasion may have been caused by the South American–African plate colliding with the southern margin of North America. As we have already noted, however, the faults had been in place since Precambrian time, and were merely reacting to another great surge of energy. Whatever the cause, the effects were very real.

A look at a map of the ancestral Rocky Mountains shows the distribution of mountain ranges in Pennsylvanian time was similar to present-day Colorado geography. The Uncompahgre and San Luis uplifts in southwestern Colorado lie along the wrench fault zone. To the east, the Wet Mountains, Sawatch, and Gore ranges form the central uplifts, rising from northward

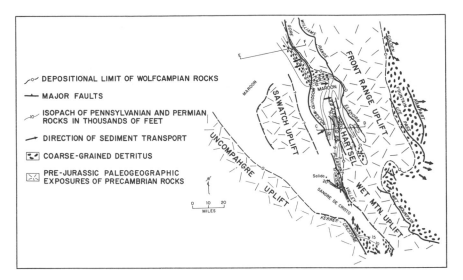

Fig. 8. The southern Rocky Mountain region east of the San Juan Mountains, showing the regional relationships of the uplifts and adjacent basins of the ancestral Rocky Mountains during Pennsylvanian and early Permian time. The ancient uplifts are precursors to the various ranges seen today. (From R.H. Devoto 1972)

horsetail splays off of the wrench fault zone, with the Front Range bounding the mountainous region on the east. The San Luis Uplift constitutes the ancient highlands of the Grenadier and Snelfels fault blocks. The Uncompahgre Uplift occurs just north of the San Juan Mountains along the present-day Uncompahgre Plateau, and is offset toward the east by faults just north of Ridgeway.

Major down-faulted basins alternate between the uplifts. The Central Colorado Trough, with its smaller subsidiary uplifts and basins, lies between the ancestral Front Range and Uncompahgre Uplift, and expands northwestward to form the larger Eagle Basin. Southwest of the Uncompahgre highland, the large and important Paradox Basin subsided rapidly in middle Pennsylvanian time. Salt was deposited in both the Eagle and Paradox basins; the Paradox contains considerably more than 4,000 feet of bedded salt in cyclic deposits. The southeastern corner of the Paradox Basin is exposed in Hermosa Mountain, where thick, black shale containing a gypsum bed occurs near the village of Hermosa. A deep well drilled just west of Durango encountered more than 100 feet of salt at that stratigraphic position in the section.

San Luis Uplift

Sandstones containing early to middle Pennsylvanian fossils occur in north-central New Mexico, where they are called the Sandia Formation. Someone, back in the good old days, believed that the sand came from the north, probably near the present-day San Luis Valley and San Luis Peak, and named the proposed highland the San Luis Uplift. No one seems to know exactly who started the notion, nor when, but the term has been applied for decades without knowing exactly where the San Luis Uplift is located. An 800-foot-thick pile of similar sandstone occurs at the base of Hermosa Mountain. As the thick sandstone has a very limited geographic distribution, it is believed to be an ancient delta. It was only recently acknowledged that these sandstones, both the Hermosa Mountain and Sandia deposits, more likely came from our old friends, the Grenadier and Sneffels fault blocks. If that is truly the case, these uplifts of Precambrian quartzite and granite constitute the long-lost San Luis Uplift. It is separated from the Uncompahgre Uplift by a down-faulted block (graben), and is older than the larger highland. Once again the ancient fault blocks in the San Juan Mountains take on an unexpected significance.

Hermosa Group

Red soils of the Molas Formation formed on the weathered surface of the Leadville Formation in late Mississippian and early Pennsylvanian time and separate the Leadville Formation from overlying rocks of Pennsylvanian age. This younger series of cyclic sandstones and shales alternating with beds of limestone is best seen in Hermosa Mountain and the Hermosa Cliffs north of Durango. The word *hermosa* is Spanish for "beautiful,"

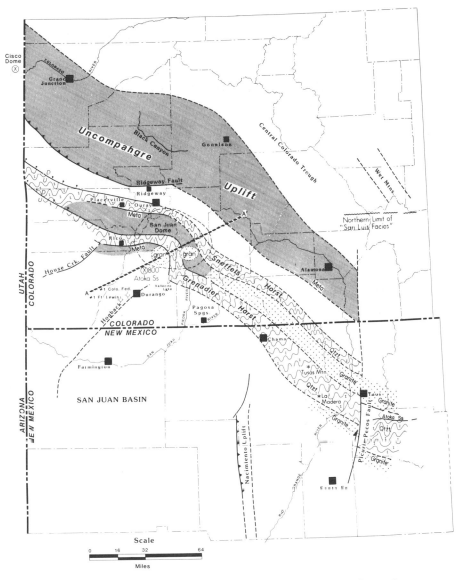

Fig. 9. Basement fault blocks in southwestern Colorado and
northern New Mexico. The Uncompahgre fault block is composed
of metamorphic rocks, and the Sneffels and Grenadier fault blocks
are predominantly quartzite. Solid lines represent faults seen at the
surface, and dashed lines show the inferred extension of these faults
where they are not exposed.

a most appropriate name for these scenic cliffs. Originally the rocks exposed here were named the Hermosa Formation, but further study revealed that they are more complicated than expected and need more detailed classification. They are now included in the Hermosa Group consisting of three formations: (1) the lower Pinkerton Trail Formation, (2) intermediate rocks, including the rock salt, called the Paradox Formation, and (3) the upper part that forms the high Hermosa Cliffs, called the Honaker Trail Formation.

Red shale of the Molas Formation grades upward into thin limestones and shales of the Pinkerton Trail Formation. Springs issuing from the east side of Hermosa Mountain were formerly known as Pinkerton Hot Springs, and a path leading from there to the top of Hermosa Mountain was called Pinkerton Trail, the type section of the formation. Roadcuts were recently made at the entrance to Tamarron Resort, providing better and more accessible exposures of the formation. The rocks represent the first invasion of Pennsylvanian seas into the region and serve to separate the Molas Formation from the overlying Paradox Formation.

The previously mentioned 800-foot-thick local pile of deltaic sandstone overlies the Pinkerton Trail Formation in Hermosa Mountain. Although it is of importance in understanding the geologic history of the region, the sandstone is of such limited geographic extent that it has never been named. By definition, it lies above the Pinkerton Trail and below the Paradox Formations, and belongs to neither. Those who wish to refer to the sandstone have called it the San Luis facies, an informal name.

Thick, black shale and a single bed of gypsum rest on the maverick sandstone in Hermosa Mountain. These rocks were deposited on the shelf adjacent to thick salt beds in the Paradox Basin to the northwest, and are called the Paradox Formation. The formation is dull and drab in the San Juan Mountains, but all that salt is important to the geology in and near Canyonlands Country in the vicinity of Moab, Utah. Recognizable beds of the Paradox thin northward and are not seen in Hermosa Cliffs exposures, because talus from the high cliffs obscures the soft-weathering shales.

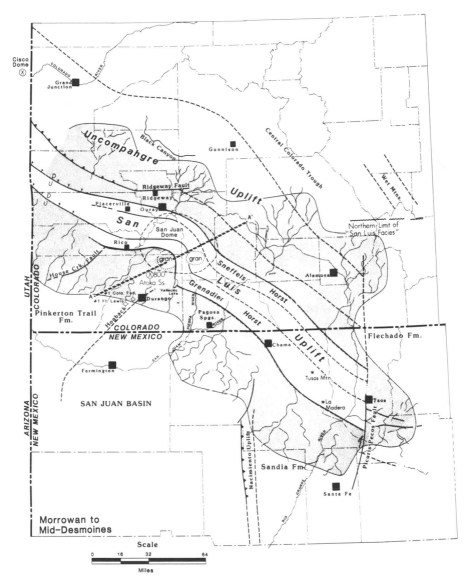

Fig. 10. Distribution of early to middle Pennsylvanian sandstones
(stippled areas) derived from the Grenadier and Sneffels fault
blocks, known collectively as the San Luis Uplift.

Rocks of the Hermosa Group showing considerable drag along the Snowdon fault north of Coal Bank Pass.

Thinly interlayered gray sandstones, shales, and limestones form an impressive escarpment, the Hermosa Cliffs, all the way from Hermosa Mountain northward to Coal Bank Pass. Rocks of the Hermosa Group form the low cliffs and shoulder of Engineer Mountain west of the pass. These rocks are included in the Honaker Trail Formation, even though they all change laterally toward the northwest into Paradox salt. The 2,500-foot-thick section of cyclically interbedded marine- and stream-deposited sediments is down-faulted along the Coal Bank Pass fault, and it forms the gray rolling hillsides northward to the vicinity of Molas Lake. In this area, sandstone beds deposited by streams alternate abruptly with shallow marine limestones as a result of the global sea level fluctuations discussed earlier. Here, too, Honaker Trail strata rest on Devonian and older rocks, where early Pennsylvanian erosion stripped the top of the San Luis Uplift, our Grenadier and Sneffels fault blocks. Sandstones in the Honaker Trail were derived from early stages of uplift on the Uncompahgre Uplift to the north and carried here to the

Syncline (down-fold) in rocks of the Hermosa Group as seen from the Lime Creek Burn overlook between Coal Bank and Molas passes; Snowdon Peak is barely visible at top. The structure formed as a result of drag along the Snowdon fault (at the right margin of the photograph) and drape over an igneous intrusive body, just out of the view at the left.

ancient shorelines by rivers. The formation is again exposed at Ouray, on the north flank of the San Juan dome, but the limestones are very thin and the sandstones very thick due to proximity to the Uncompahgre source area.

The wrench faults of the San Juan Mountains were again playing their little tricks during deposition of the Pennsylvanian rocks. Most obvious is a fault that crosses U.S. Highway 550 between Coal Bank and Molas passes near Lime Creek. Drag along the fault has caused a noticeably sharp up-fold in the rocks, but this could have happened much later in geologic history. However, Pennsylvanian rocks rest directly on Precambrian quartzite, indicating that the fault block was high in Pennsylvanian time, and an unconformity within Pennsylva-

A local angular unconformity within rocks of the Hermosa Group along U.S. Highway 550 north of Coal Bank Pass. Strata behind the white signpost were deposited and dragged up along the Snowdon fault, which lies in the wooded area beyond the roadcuts, and then bevelled by erosion prior to deposition of the sandstone layer visible at the top of the signpost. The entire section was then dragged up to the fault at some later time.

nian rocks tells us that there was Pennsylvanian movement as well. Older Hermosa beds were bent up toward the fault, and then they were leveled by erosion before younger Hermosa beds were deposited on the unconformity. The entire section was bent up to the fault again at some later time. There are other subtle hints that the faults were active in Pennsylvanian time, but this is the best, most clearly seen evidence.

Rico

A long-standing argument persists regarding where in the layered rocks to place the Pennsylvanian-Permian time boundary in the San Juan Mountains and Colorado Plateau.

In the late 1800s, Whitman Cross and his crew were mapping

the geology of the San Juan Mountains for the U.S. Geological Survey and had trouble separating rocks of the two geologic periods in the Rico Quadrangle on the west side of the range. (*Rico* means "rich" in Spanish, and the name was given to the village and mining district because of its silver production in those days.) The rock layers in question are not well exposed in the area, and in his dilemma, Cross named the Rico Formation specifically for the transitional beds between marine rocks of Pennsylvanian age below and non-marine rocks of Permian age above, paraphrasing the original definition. This produced a formation with gradational contacts both above and below, a situation which makes it almost impossible to map or study the formation: you can't find it!

We now know that the top of the Pennsylvanian Hermosa Group is an erosional surface, an unconformity, in southwestern Colorado and much of southeastern Utah, and that the contact is not gradational. Only six or seven miles east of the Rico Quadrangle, near Engineer Mountain, rocks of the Hermosa Group are again exposed. Here the rocks are at or above timberline, where they are not obscured by soil and tree cover. In this area, the contact between the Hermosa and red sandstone of the Cutler Formation is an erosional surface. The contact is everywhere sharp and definitely not gradational, and furthermore, the Coal Bank fault luckily moved once again, creating a local angular unconformity at the Hermosa-Cutler contact. The Pennsylvanian Hermosa section north of the fault was uplifted, tilted, and eroded before the red rocks, believed to be Permian in age, were deposited. Pebbles of these eroded rocks were deposited on the down-thrown side of the fault, forming a thick limestone conglomerate at the base of the upper peak of Engineer Mountain, just south of the fault.

In brief, transitional rocks, grading from the marine Pennsylvanian age Hermosa Group into the nonmarine Cutler Formation, do not seem to exist in the San Juan Mountains, and thus no Rico Formation is present as originally defined.

Big Red

O ne of the most memorable traits of the American Southwest is that the rocks are colorful. Red rocks dominate the scenery across the Colorado Plateau (indeed, *colorado* is Spanish for "colorful" or "red"), and they are not uncommon in the southern Rocky Mountains. A noteworthy example is the Maroon Bells, 14,000-foot-high peaks near Aspen, Colorado. Nearly all of the red scenery is due to sedimentary rocks of Pennsylvanian and Permian age in which the original sediments were derived from the ancestral Rocky Mountains.

Red pigmentation is due to iron oxide, usually hematite, in the mud or matrix of the sedimentary rock. Basement rocks that supplied the sediments from the ancient uplifts are largely metamorphic rocks (gneisses and schists), and granite, containing significant proportions of ferromagnesian minerals, such as hornblende, augite, and chlorite. When these minerals are deposited and weathered in an arid environment, as here in Pennsylvanian-Permian times, they break down chemically to form hematite, clay, and calcite, among other things. Hematite provides the reddish brown stain, clay forms the matrix, and calcite acts as the cement to change drab sediments into colorful rocks.

Rivers that drained the west flank of the Uncompahgre Uplift

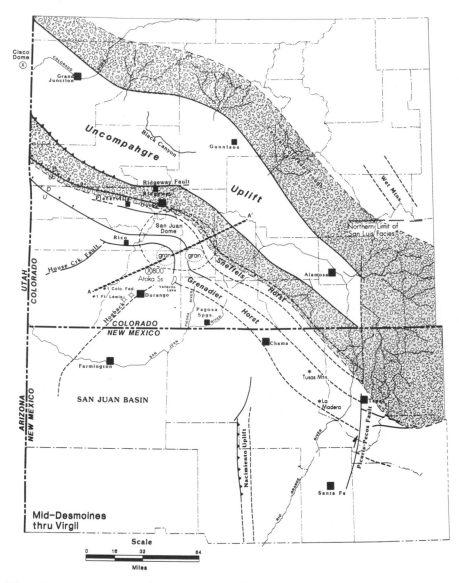

Fig. 11. Distribution of coarse-grained arkosic sandstone and conglomerate derived from the Uncompahgre uplift in middle to late Pennsylvanian time. The thick accumulations of coarse sediments were deposited mainly in the deep downfaulted trough formed adjacent to the southwest flank of the Uncompahgre Uplift.

carried copious amounts of mud, sand, and gravel that were rich in iron-bearing minerals. Much of the sediment was dumped immediately as the rivers debouched from the mountains onto the low plains of the eastern Paradox Basin, but finer silts and clays were transported hundreds of miles to the west. Sediments began accumulating even as the uplift was rising in middle Pennsylvanian time and continued into the lower Permian. The stagnant sea of the Paradox Basin had by then been crowded to the west by the great onslaught of river sediments that accumulated at the eastern shoreline. Chemical weathering attacked the sediments almost immediately, and red coloration developed rapidly—at least in geologic time. These accumulations west of the Uncompahgre Uplift are called the Cutler Formation. Coarse-grained sandstones and conglomerates attain thicknesses of more than 12,000 feet near the west face of the uplift, much of which is late Pennsylvanian in age, as shown by deep drilling. Farther west, the rocks thin. There the rocks of lower Permian age are called the Cutler Group, containing various named formations, such as the Halgaito Shale, Cedar Mesa Sandstone, Organ Rock Shale, and De Chelly Sandstone in Monument Valley.

Cutler Formation

Red rocks of the Cutler Formation cap the gray Hermosa Group in Hermosa Mountain and dip southward down to and under the floor of the Animas Valley north of Durango. Here the formation consists of a 2,500-foot thickness of sandstone and shale, believed to be Permian. No fossils have been found in the stream-deposited sedimentary rocks, so their age is inferred from regional relationships.

The formation's name is from Cutler Creek, five miles north of Ouray, where massive course-grained sandstone and conglomerate dominate the valley of Uncompahgre Creek. It is not possible to measure the thickness of the formation at that locality because much of the formation is underground. Uplift along the Sneffels fault block tilted the rocks, and pre-Triassic erosion removed the upper beds, further complicating the situa-

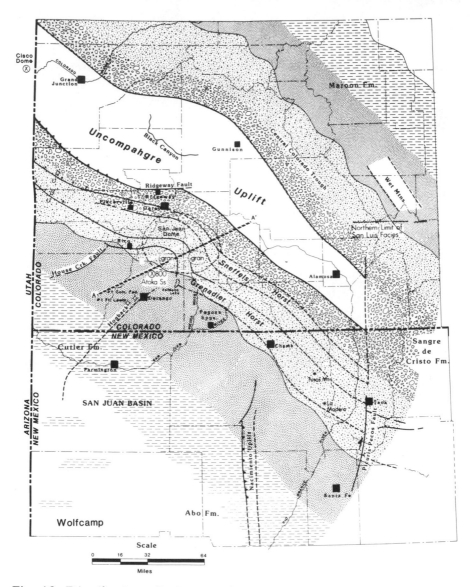

Fig. 12. Distribution of arkosic sediments derived from the Uncompahgre Uplift in early Pennsylvanian time. As shown by the map patterns, the coarsest sediments were deposited close to the Uncompahgre source area, and the deposits become finer-grained farther away from the uplift. Although faults of the Grenadier and Sneffels fault blocks were reactivated during this time, the Cutler sediments effectively buried those fault blocks. These deposits are known by different names in different areas, as indicated on the map.

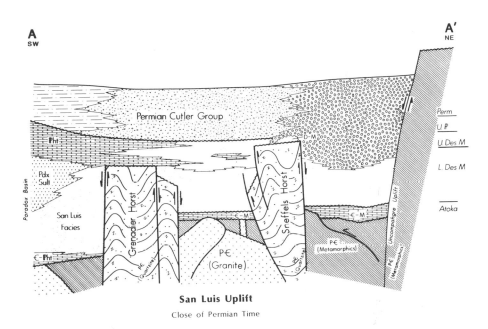

San Luis Uplift

Close of Permian Time

Fig. 13. Schematic cross-section showing the relationships between the Grenadier and Sneffels fault blocks (San Luis uplift) and the somewhat younger Uncompahgre uplift. The location of the cross-section is shown in Figs. 9–12 as the dashed line **A—A.** PC = Precambrian; **C–M** = Cambrian to Mississippian; **C–Pht** = Cambrian to Pennsylvanian; **D–M** = Devonian to Mississippian; **Pdx salt** = Paradox salt.

tion. The tilting and erosional event created an angular unconformity at the base of the Triassic Dolores Formation that may be seen in upper Cutler Creek and high in the cliffs above the town of Ouray.

Other than in the several valleys carved into the flanks of the dome, such as Vallecito Creek, the Pine River, and the Dolores River near Rico, Cutler red beds have been stripped from the crest of the San Juan Mountains by later erosion. Remnants of the Cutler may be seen at the bases of the high peaks of Engineer and Graysill mountains and beneath volcanic rocks high above and to the west of Molas Pass.

Because of this mass stripping of the formation from the high country, it is not possible to determine whether there was movement on the basement faults during Permian time, except for the exposures at Ouray. Certainly there the Sneffels fault block was uplifted after, and perhaps during, deposition of the Cutler Formation. This would be the last recorded movement of any significance on the wrench faults. The stresses in the earth's crust that caused the faults' strange antics faded and died by the close of Permian time. Only memories remain of the important faults that formed the ancestral Rocky Mountains and shaped the destiny of the Colorado Plateau. There are still faint murmurings from slight movements on the faults in the form of minor earthquakes, but their heyday is long past.

The Dull Days

M any million years of geologic time passed after deposition of the Cutler Formation without leaving a
record in the rocks. There are no strata of middle or late Permian
age preserved in the San Juan Mountains or Colorado Plateau,
and the nearest rocks of early Triassic age, the Moenkopi Formation, are found in Utah. Perhaps the fault blocks were active
again, but there is no way to know. The entire Colorado Plateau
and southern Rocky Mountain provinces probably lay low and
dormant. If any sediments were deposited, they were removed
by erosion before red beds of the late Triassic Dolores Formation were laid down.

Triassic Time

When Whitman Cross mapped the geology in the western
San Juan Mountains in the late 1890s, he included the entire
section of red rocks in his Dolores Formation. Not until he had
worked his way northward to the Ouray Quadrangle and seen
the angular unconformity in the canyon of Cutler Creek did he
realized that two different rock units were present. He then
distinguished the Cutler from the overlying Dolores red beds.

Where the unconformity is not angular, as in the Animas Valley at the northern outskirts of Durango, it is difficult to separate the two formations. Yet the gap in the geologic record is present, distinguishable only by a channel-filling sandstone.

Both formations, the Cutler and the Dolores, consist of dark reddish brown sandstones and shales, as the sediments all came from the same source area, the Uncompahgre Uplift. However, by Triassic time the mountainous region had been worn down to low, hilly country by millions of years of erosion, a mere shadow of its former configuration, and the sediments produced were much finer grained than before. Streams draining the uplift were more sluggish now and could only carry mud and silt-size sediments. Thus, grain size is the chief distinguishing factor. Fossil remains of palm fronds have been found in the western San Juan Mountains, indicating that the climate was warm and moist here in late Triassic time. Where the formation loses most of its red color and becomes a varicolored shale to the west and north, it is called the Chinle Formation. That name is also used for red beds in New Mexico and Arizona. Shales of the Chinle actually lie directly on the basement on the Uncompahgre Uplift, as shown especially well at Colorado National Monument west of Grand Junction, burying the source rocks for all time.

Because of the later erosional stripping of the San Juan Dome, the Dolores Formation is found only along the distal margins of the high country. It is best seen in canyon walls of the larger tributary streams that radiate from the uplift, such as in the Animas Valley just north of Durango and north of Ouray.

Jurassic Rocks

Red rocks of the Dolores Formation change abruptly upward into the overlying white cliffs of the Entrada Sandstone. The Entrada is the lower of two prominent white sandstones above the red beds just north of Durango. A thin, reddish colored sandstone occurs at the base of the cliff. Some geologists believe that this is a far eastern extension of the Wingate Sandstone of the Colorado Plateau, but that seems unlikely. The remainder of the white cliff is a very clean sandstone generally considered to have been deposited as a windblown (eolian) dune sand. A regionally developed erosional surface, known as the J-2 Unconformity, occurs at the base of the Entrada over most of the Colorado Plateau to the west.

An erosional pinnacle of Entrada Sandstone on the north edge of Durango, known as X-Rock for a pair of X-shaped fractures on its face, is a favorite training ground for local rock climbers. The formation is also prominent along the Dolores River near Stoner and forms a distinctive cliff north of Ouray. It is the same layer of sandstone that contains myriad natural arches in Arches National Park near Moab, Utah.

A thin limestone bed rests on the Entrada Sandstone. It is only a foot or two thick at Durango, making a mere pencil-line when viewed from the Animas Valley. It is called the Pony Express Limestone, named for a mine near Ouray where it is a little thicker. The rock is everywhere very dark gray and greasy in appearance because it contains finely disseminated organic matter. Many years of searching for clues as to the origin of the formation have proved fruitless. Some believe that it was deposited in a large lake, others that it represents a long arm of the sea. The only fossils found to date are a kind of fish that are undiagnostic, so we haven't a clue as to which story is correct. This is the same layer of rock known as the Todilto Formation in New Mexico.

A tree-covered slope separates the two white sandstone cliffs above the Pony Express Limestone north of Durango. In rare exposures where the soil and vegetation don't completely hide the rock, it is found to be another reddish colored shale called the Wanakah Formation (pronounced with emphasis on "na"). It was named for another mine near Ouray. Although the Wanakah was originally believed to be an extension of the Summerville Formation of the Colorado Plateau to the west, detailed studies now show that correlation to be incorrect.

Yet another sandstone forms a higher prominent white cliff in the valley walls. This one, called the Junction Creek Sandstone for exposures in the tributary near Durango, is also probably of a windblown origin. It is an eastward extension of the Bluff Sandstone of southeastern Utah.

A greenish gray, slope-forming shale called the Morrison Formation tops off the Jurassic section in the fringes of the San Juan Mountains. The formation is widespread geographically, blanketing the Colorado Plateau and Rocky Mountains provinces. The name is derived from exposures at Morrison, Colorado, on the east flank of the Rockies near Denver. The sandstones and shales of the Morrison were deposited by a broad network of rivers and lakes in latest Jurassic time. Many complete dinosaur fossils have been excavated from the Morrison at Colorado National Monument near Grand Junction, at Dinosaur National Monument near Vernal, Utah, and the Cleveland-Lloyd Quarry south of Price, Utah. Nearly complete skeletons from the Morrison Formation decorate some of the finest museums throughout the world. The formation also hosts many of the largest uranium deposits at various places across the Colorado Plateau. The Morrison Formation forms long slopes beneath the caprock of Animas City Mountain on the north edge of Durango.

Cretaceous Seas

As if all that weren't enough, the seas flooded the interior of the continent once again in Cretaceous time. It all began in southwestern Colorado when the shoreline came crawling over the flat landscape from the northeast, intermixing stream deposits, coal formed in coastal swamps, and beach sands in what is called the Dakota Sandstone. It is best seen as the southward-sloping caprock to Animas City Mountain at the north city limits of Durango.

Did we just say the shoreline came in from the northeast? That's right. Until now the main seaway lay to the west in western Utah and Nevada, but in Jurassic time a great wave of mountain-building forces rammed the continent from the west, forming great mountain ranges by thrust faulting. It is thought that the catastrophe was caused by the North American continent overriding sea floor rocks of the Pacific Ocean. A seaway divided the North American continent and extended from the Gulf of Mexico through central Canada to northern Alaska in late Cretaceous time. Untold thousands of cubic miles of sediment washed from the newly formed mountain masses to the west, and further crowded back the displaced sea.

The results of all this sediment being dumped into the seaway may be seen around the towns of Durango, Cortez, and Grand Junction. Shoreline sandstones are dull tan colored, but the open marine muds formed the thick, dark gray or even black, very drab shales so characteristic of these regions. The shales are black because they contain an abundance of organic material deposited in the sea, much of which has turned to oil over the eons. When the organic material is deeply weathered, oxidation forms a sickly yellow hue on the otherwise dark gray surface.

(No, these are not the famed "oil shales"—which are neither shales nor contain true oil—but the oily source rocks of petroleum. If you heat some of the crushed shale in a test tube, a ring of true oil will form above the rock. In the case of oil shale, the rocks are actually shaly dolomite that contain kerogen, a bituminous material that must be heated and hydrogenated to form petroleum.)

After the shoreline passed through the area the first time, leaving behind the Dakota Sandstone, waters deepened and offshore mud was deposited that would become the Mancos Shale. This is seen as the long, black shale slopes surrounding Durango, named for similar exposures near Mancos, Colorado. The shale contains abundant bentonite, a clay with a high shrink-swell capacity, formed from the alteration of volcanic ash from volcanoes far to the west. It makes a very unsuitable base upon which to build highways, airports, or houses, as they tend to sink out of sight every time it rains hard. It is wise to stay away from unpaved roads on Mancos Shale surfaces and to be wary of paved roads that buckle and sink or slide down hillsides when wet. A Durango man once testified at a land use hearing that he wasn't worried about his house, but he was afraid that his entire lot would slide down the hill. The Mancos Shale is 2,000–4,000 feet thick and weathers to soft slopes and broad valleys. Conse-

Aerial view of Durango, Colorado, nestled in the foothills of the La Plata Mountains. The badlands just beyond the city are in the Mancos Shale, capped by the Point Lookout Sandstone of the Mesaverde Group, all of late Cretaceous age. The high mountains are late Paleozoic sedimentary rocks intruded by igneous stocks of Tertiary age. The rounded flat, right of center, is the site of Fort Lewis College.

quently, most towns and main highways in the region are constructed on this relatively flat topography. Shark teeth, a variety of cephalopods, and many kinds of microfossils may be found in the Mancos Shale.

Relative sea level rose and fell several times during the late Cretaceous time, and shorelines waxed and waned accordingly. When the shore of the Mancos Sea first pulled back toward the northeast, beach sands of the Point Lookout Sandstone of the Mesaverde Group (don't ask why Mesa Verde is written "Mesaverde") were deposited. An erosional remnant of the formation is seen capping Perins Peak west of Durango and above the entry road to Mesa Verde National Park. As the beach marched northeastward, coastal swamps formed on the new landscape, producing today's coal seen along the highway leading toward Cortez from Durango. The deposits are now called the Menefee Formation. The sea didn't stay away for long, and as it returned, deposited more beach sands of the Cliff House Sandstone. Rocks of the Point Lookout, Menefee, and Cliff House formations comprise the Mesaverde Group and hold up the prominent cliffs in Mesa Verde National Park and the hogback ridges that extend from near Shiprock, New Mexico, past Durango to near Pagosa Springs, Colorado.

As deeper marine waters followed the Cliff House beach into the region, another marine mud was deposited exactly like the Mancos Shale. The thick, black shales, seen south of Durango, are called the Lewis Shale. By now the basin margin was filled with sediments, and the beach headed back to the east, this time depositing the Pictured Cliffs Sandstone that makes the prominent sandstone cliffs south of Durango. Rocks above the Pictured Cliffs Sandstone are deposits from northeastward-flowing streams and coal of the Kirtland-Fruitland Formations. The McDermott purplish conglomeratic beds were formed by dumping of sediments derived from the uplift of the San Juan Dome to the north in latest Cretaceous and early Tertiary times.

The entire 16,000-foot-thick section of sedimentary rocks exposed in the Animas Valley dips southward away from the San Juan Dome, diving deep underground into the San Juan Basin of northwest New Mexico. The dividing line between the uplift and basin is arbitrarily placed at the line of sandstone hogback ridges. Each of the Cretaceous sandstones produces prolific natural gas, making the San Juan a giant gas-producing basin.

Chapter 8
Uplift

W hen the late Cretaceous seas quietly departed toward the east, it was largely at the insistence of the Laramide orogeny. Until then, the area that would become southwestern Colorado was a low, very flat surface, first under seawater and later exposed as a broad plain. There were no mountains, not even low hills, east of the thrust-faulted ranges of western Utah.

The onset of great compressional forces in the earth's crust rolling in from the west began in Nevada in Jurassic time, but increased in intensity and flowed eastward during the Cretaceous. By the close of marine sedimentation in late Cretaceous time, the force field had reached the region now known as the Colorado Plateau. The layered rocks buckled, folded, and were uplifted along preexisting lines of weakness that were the legacy of Precambrian rifting. Great folds and uplifts, such as the San Rafael Swell of north-central Utah, the Monument Upwarp of southeastern Utah and northern Arizona, and the Kaibab Uplift of Grand Canyon fame, buckled and groaned into major structures behind the retreating sea. Southwestern Colorado, not to be outdone by all this excitement, began to rise, and a great circular dome formed. This episode of mountain-building is known as the Laramide orogeny. It began in latest Cretaceous time and continued into the early days of the Tertiary Period, forming the Colorado Plateau and Rocky Mountains as we know them today. The San Juan Mountains were on the rise.

Most Laramide structures are elongate uplifts that trend generally north-south, at right angles to the easterly-directed earth forces. On the contrary, as we already know, the San Juan country buckled into a unique circular uplift. This discrepancy in shape is because other uplifts formed above linear basement faults that already were partly oriented across the force field, but the San Juan basement faults were sharply kinked and cored by the location of the massive Precambrian Eolus Granite. Such a basement fabric could do nothing but rise to a dome culminating over the ancient knot.

Even as the dome began to rise, erosion took command. It is well known that higher ground is subject to more intense erosion than lower country. This is because storms concentrate their intensity over high country, and runoff has steeper courses to follow. The San Juan Dome was no exception. By the end of the Cretaceous Period, a purple bed of conglomerate was already deposited in the northern San Juan Basin, which had begun to sag relative to the San Juan Dome. This deposit, the McDermott Formation, is conspicuous south of Durango. Surprisingly, the boulders in the conglomerate are composed of igneous rock of a type not yet found in place in the region, although it is believed to have been located somewhere in the La Plata Mountains west of Durango. Then stream-deposited sandstones and shales of the Ojo Alamo, Animas, Nacimiento, and San Jose Formations filled the basin to the south as uplift of the dome intensified.

At the culmination of uplift, in early Tertiary time, Precambrian rocks at the crest of the San Juan Mountains were at least 20,000 feet higher than those at the bottom of the adjacent San Juan and Paradox basins. How's that for an uplift? Erosion had already exhumed the apex of the dome, and older Paleozoic and Precambrian rocks were exposed. This early erosional episode is recorded in the Telluride Conglomerate. It rests with angular discordance on all older rocks down to the basement, and the nature of the boulders tells the story well. Boulders at the base of the formation in the northern San Juan Mountains consist of sedimentary rocks of Mesozoic age and grade upward through Paleozoic limestone cobbles, with Precambrian quartzite and granite pebbles occurring only near the top. In other words, the erosional fragments occur in reverse stratigraphic order. Erosion had begun when the highest, youngest rocks were being affected, and as erosion continued to attack deeper and older rocks, they contributed to the conglomerate in order. The conglomerate is believed to be of early Tertiary age.

Then the entire Colorado Plateau and Rocky Mountains, indeed the whole interior of the continent, was bodily uplifted another 5,000 feet or so, touching off an intense convulsion.

Not a Pretty Sight

Volcanoes broke out along the basement faults, spewing several thousand feet of lavas and ash onto the top and eastern flank of the San Juan dome. Throats of the volcanoes are now exposed in the Silverton, Creede, Lake City, and other calderas in the eastern San Juans. The resulting holocaust, several million years of violent volcanic eruptions, deposited the thick San Juan Volcanic Series. Lavas and ash completely buried older rocks of the eastern San Juan Mountains to considerable depth, and capped many of the high peaks near Silverton, such as Kendall Mountain, Grand Turk, Sultan, and Grizzly peaks.

Volcanoes first broke the surface and began disgorging ash and other ejecta about 40 million years ago. Andesitic lava flows soon followed, and low, rounded volcanoes, not unlike those in the Hawaiian Islands today, began to form. Flows from the several stratovolcanoes merged to form a broad volcanic plateau in the region of the eastern San Juan Mountains about 30 million years ago. It was exactly then that violent eruptions poured Vesuvius-like, red-hot, gas-laden ash flows from five separate calderas, first in the northeastern and southern parts of the volcanic plateau and a couple of million years later in central and western areas. These include the Ute Creek, Lost Lake, San Juan, Uncompahgre, and Silverton calderas.

With repeated cataclysmic eruptions, volcanoes collapsed in

Lizard Head, at Lizard Head Pass, is comprised of Telluride Conglomerate in the lower cliff, with rocks of the San Juan Volcanic Series in the upper spire. Although tempting to rock climbers, the upper pitch is very crumbly, rotten rock and is highly dangerous.

the central area, forming eight calderas in less than approximately 1.5 million years. The violence gradually subsided and basaltic flows emanated from the volcanic centers, except in the east, where the Lake City caldera collapsed and formed ash deposits in the vicinity of present-day Sunshine Peak about 23 million years ago. In all, 18 calderas (collapsed volcanoes) formed above a shallow molten intrusive magma beneath the eastern San Juan Mountains. The calderas were partially filled with ash and debris flows by later eruptions. Continued doming, eruptions, and collapse formed new calderas within older

Chapter Eight

calderas, and faulting connected the Silverton and Lake City centers, further complicating the issue. As volcanic activity subsided over a period of ten million years or so, mineralized fluids seeped through myriad fractures and fissures, depositing rich veins of precious ore.

Some intrusive stocks and sills squeezed into sedimentary rocks in the San Juan Mountains. For example, the capping, nearly white rocks on Engineer and Graysill mountains are intrusive sills of probable Tertiary age. At about the same time, intrusive igneous bodies were elbowing their way into the earth's crust in the isolated high ranges to the west. Fortunately, at least for the primitive horses, camels, and tigers that roamed the nearby plains, these intrusions did not reach the surface to form volcanoes. The irregularly shaped intrusive bodies have now been denuded by erosion to form prominent landmarks, such as the La Plata, Ute, and La Sal mountains, across the Colorado Plateau.

Riches

Highly mineralized juices accompanied and followed this intense volcanic activity, emplacing innumerable deposits of metaliferous minerals in fractures formed by the eruptions. Veins containing rich ores of gold, silver, copper, lead, and zinc radiate from the volcanic necks and other igneous bodies. These deposits became paramount in the history of the San Juan and La Plata mountains in the late 1800s and early 1900s.

This period was followed by a new cycle of erosion, working first to strip away much of the gray, volcanic deposits and then to complete the alpine architecture.

Chapter 9

Cenozoic Strip Tease

T he San Juan Mountains were already ravaged by torrential streams and quite lofty by the end of Tertiary time. Not only was the crest of the range sharply sculpted, but deep canyons radiated from the highlands. Still, the San Juans had little character—the job was not quite completed. The finishing touches to form a truly alpine scene would have to come from glacial erosion. Fortunately, the great Ice Age occurred in the last million years or so, just in the nick of time.

The Ice Man

No one knows exactly what happened to cause it, but excessive ice began to pile up in the polar regions of the earth only a couple of million years ago, more or less contemporary with the development of modern humankind. Ocean currents changed and the climate became noticeably cooler and more moist. It snowed abundantly, more than could be melted, and glaciers formed. The great Ice Age, or Pleistocene Epoch, was under way.

Continental glaciers, the kind that blanket Greenland and the polar regions today, gradually increased in size until large parts of North America (and other continents) were under hundreds or thousands of feet of creeping blue ice. Deposits left by the great ice sheets are found as far south as Kansas, forming hummocky, rocky cover over much of Canada and the northern United States. It is not surprising that with all this going on, the higher mountain regions of the world became glaciated as well, even those much farther south than the continental glaciers extended. The San Juan Mountains are excellent examples of this so-called alpine glaciation.

San Juan Ice Cap

Permanent snowfields began to build up in the high San Juan Mountains in the vicinity of Silverton, when more snow fell each year than could melt during the summers. As the annual layers accumulated, older snow packs recrystallized and compressed, gradually changing to ice. The ice finally reached a critical thickness, probably a couple of hundred feet, and began to creep downhill under its own weight and the pull of gravity. When ice actually begins to flow, it becomes an official glacier. The ice built up to several hundred feet in thickness in the vicinity of the Needles, Grenadier, and Silverton ranges, and flowed outward from the ice cap along the already established river canyons that radiated from the high country. The higher peaks, including Engineer Mountain and Potato Hill near Coal Bank Pass, stood high and dry, forming what are called *nunataks,* or islands rising above the ice. Lower, now rounded hills and slopes were deeply buried. Major valley glaciers flowed from the mountains in the Animas Valley, at Telluride, at Ouray on the west side, and at Lake City to the east.

Plucking and Scraping

How is it possible to know all this? Live glaciers produce distinctive erosional features that form by no other process. Rivers erode their canyons by downward cutting only, thus forming V-shaped canyons; even the small trickles at the headwaters cut V-shaped gullies. Glaciers, on the other hand, carry rock debris picked up when ice freezes around boulders at its head, base, and sides, and some talus cascades onto the sides of the glacier from adjacent cliffs. The boulders are carried along on the glacier's down-valley trek, serving as grinding tools at the base and sides of the ice. Thus, glaciers widen their canyons as they cut downward, forming U-shaped valleys. The wide-floored valleys of the Animas River north of Durango, at Telluride, at Ironton Park south of Ouray, and the valley of Mineral Creek between Silverton and Red Mountain Pass, are classic examples of glacial erosion.

There are other telltale signs of glacial erosion. Ice freezes around boulders and in rock fractures at the head of a glacier, and when the ice moves, it plucks these boulders from the mountainside and carries them away. The result is a bowl-shaped hollow, called a *cirque,* formed on the mountainside. Several cirques are visible from Molas Pass. The most obvious are aligned beneath the high ridge to the northeast from Kendall Mountain south to Whitehead Gulch. Another example is on the distant mountain to the north beyond Silverton. When the glacier finally melts from the cirque, a small lake, called a *tarn,* is often formed in the hollowed-out base of the cirque.

If a small glacier is tributary to a larger ice stream, the valley of the larger glacier will be cut the deepest. When the glaciers melt, the smaller tributary valley is left perched above the main valley and a "hanging valley" marks the junction. Each of the cirques described above in the Silverton area is a hanging valley along the main Animas glacial valley. An unusual variety of hanging valley occurs in the Falls Creek area just northwest of Durango. There, a small glacier came down Hermosa Creek and merged laterally with the main Animas glacier. The hanging valley of the Hermosa Creek tributary glacier is a perched bench above and parallel to the west wall of the Animas Valley.

If cirques form on three or more sides of a mountain, chipping away at its sides, the remnant peak is often shaped like the Matterhorn in the Swiss Alps and is called a matterhorn or simply a *horn.* Pigeon and Turret peaks at the west end of the Needles Range are excellent examples of horns, as is the Golden Horn in the Silverton Range visible to the west from the mouth of South Fork of Mineral Creek between Silverton and Red Mountain Pass. Mount Sneffels, northwest of Ouray and best seen from near Dallas Divide west of Ridgeway, is another beautiful horn. Peaks of the Grenadier Range are also horns, but their shapes are somewhat altered by being upturned, thrust-faulted quartzite beds.

Rocks dragged along under and at the sides of a glacier scrape underlying bedrock to polish and striate, or gouge, the surface. Examples of polished and striated bedrock surfaces are abundant from Shalona Lake north of Durango to Ironton Park near Ouray.

Any combination of these erosional features in mountainous terrain indicates the former presence of glaciers. The San Juan Mountains are a showcase of such erosional features.

Glacial Garbage Dumps

As the ice melts in the lower, warmer reaches of the glacier, boulders, sand, and mud incorporated in the ice are freed and dumped randomly or in piles called *moraines.* Boulder dumps at the snout of the glacier, where the ice melts as fast as it flows, are called *terminal moraines,* and those along the sides of a glacier are *lateral moraines.* These form long ridge-like piles of loose boulders and mud that cross the glaciated valley and line the valley walls, respectively. Debris that melts out from under the glacier results in *ground moraines,* sometimes in strange shapes variously known as *drumlins, eskers,* and other unseemly names.

Moraines can be dated in a relative sense, and therefore the generalized times of glacial epochs can be determined. Where two or more moraines are preserved, the oldest are always on higher ground, since later glaciers only cut the canyon deeper and deposit their loads at the lowered levels. Moraines occur in association with outwash river plains, where meltwater is released. As younger glacial episodes leave perched moraines, outwash plains are also cut by younger, deeper canyons, and perched river terraces result. Each level of preserved moraines is accompanied down-valley by a perched outwash terrace covered with river gravels.

If there is any doubt about which moraine or terrace is the older, another highly technical method is used to make the distinction. As the boulders in the deposits are weathered, they gradually deteriorate and become soft or punky. When struck with a rock hammer, freshly deposited boulders will ring, or respond with a "clink" sound; boulders in older deposits, being more highly weathered, will make more of a "clunk" sound. People with little on their minds and nothing better to do walk around on moraines hitting boulders with hammers. They count the number of boulders that clink and those that clunk to derive the "clink:clunk ratio" of the deposit. Younger moraines have higher clink:clunk ratios than older deposits. It is no wonder that Indians in the 1800s thought geologists were crazy and wouldn't come near them! The same is true today in the San Juan Mountains with tourists and geologists.

The least accurate method in determining the age of moraines is by carbon14 dating techniques. Wood fragments and charcoal found in the deposits can be dated, but the method only works for carbon-bearing materials less than about 40,000 years old.

There are remains of three, and perhaps four, glacial moraines at Durango. Animas Valley glaciers didn't get south of town (perhaps the Diamond Belle Saloon was already using the ice for drinks). The oldest moraine deposited during the Durangoan glacial epoch has been nearly destroyed by erosion, but remnants are found along the north edge of the Durango Golf Course on College Heights. Fort Lewis College occupies its perched outwash terrace. The clink:clunk ratio is dismal for these deposits, but they are probably about 250,000–330,000 years old, approximately coeval with the so-called Illinoisian glacial epoch of the upper midcontinent.

The second oldest glacial deposits at Durango are called the Spring Creek Moraines. They are found capping intermediate-height hills along Florida Road, north of and below the Durango Moraine. Second Avenue in Durango occupies the outwash terrace associated with these moraines. Their age is believed to be the same as the Bull Lake glacial epoch of Wyoming, which has been dated at between 88,000 and 150,000 years ago, according to the clink:clunk ratio method.

Finally, two sharp morainal ridges used to occur along either side of 32nd Street in north Durango. Depending upon when one visits them, they may be in various states of ruin, thanks to municipal decisions to tear down the moraines either for the gravel deposits or to use as flattened sites for shaky housing developments. The moraines occur at valley level, lower than the other deposits, and are much younger according to their clink:clunk ratio. Radiocarbon dating suggests that the moraines are older than 16,000 years, and may be as old as 40,000–70,000 years, or the Wisconsin glacial epoch of the northern midcontinent region. Other evidence indicates that deglaciation of the San Juan Mountains was well underway by about 15,000 years ago. The northern, or up-valley, moraine is necessarily younger than the southern moraine, otherwise it would have been bulldozed by the younger glacier.

When fresh, the moraines crossed the Animas Valley, damming the valley and forming Lake Animas. The extremely flat valley floor from here north to Baker's Bridge consists of sediments deposited in this lake as the last glaciers receded. Drilling of water wells in the Animas Valley suggests that the lake sediments, derived from the melting glaciers, are several hundred feet thick.

Perched terraces formed during the major episodes of glacial melting in the San Juan Mountains are obvious downstream from Durango. In fact, the terraces and their gravels may be traced downriver through Aztec, Farmington, and Shiprock in New Mexico, and on through southeastern Utah along the course of the San Juan River all the way to Lake Powell, a distance of several hundred river miles. For the entire distance, the cobbles clearly show their San Juan Mountains origin by their rock types that include quartzite, gneiss, schist, and slate not available to erosion at any other site. Dust-size gold, known as "flour gold," carried down from the San Juan Mountains and included in the terrace gravels, caused a major gold rush near the Goosenecks of the San Juan in 1882, when more than 15,000 prospectors reportedly crowded into the canyon. However, an epitaph inscribed on a boulder in the area read, "One hundred dollars reward for the damned fool who started the gold boom."

With the melting of the last glaciers, some 15,000 years remained for river erosion to deepen the higher glaciated valleys. An obvious example is Animas Canyon just south of Silverton. If one looks south into the canyon from the west edge of town, a high U-shaped upper valley is seen to have a sharp Vshaped canyon cut into its floor. Other high mountain canyons show similar cosmetic effects.

Rock glaciers are characteristic features of the San Juan Mountains. They consist of low ridges of boulders that occur much like ice glaciers, flowing from cirques down formerly glaciated valleys, sometimes considerable distances. The boulder piles actually creep downhill at much slower rates than ice glaciers, but flow ridges on the surfaces mark patterns of movement. Although rock glaciers have been studied rather intensely, it remains unclear whether they consist of boulders creeping down-slope under their own weight, or whether they are ice glaciers that are thoroughly buried with talus. A couple of rock glaciers have been penetrated by mining and road-building activities, and they were found to have ice cores. However, it has not been possible to determine whether the ice is the flowing agent or is entirely passive. It has been speculated that the ice cores are buried remnants of Pleistocene (Ice Age) ice, but that seems doubtful. The unstable nature of the boulder piles makes very difficult climbing, much like climbing on fresh moraines.

Plate 1. Twilight Peak from just north of Coal Bank Pass. The south-bounding fault of the Grenadier fault block is along the base of the cliff at right and straight up the far side of Lime Creek to the notch just north of Twilight Peak. Rocks to the south (right) of the fault are metamorphic rocks of the Twilight Gneiss, rocks to the north (left) are quartzites and slates of the younger Precambrian Uncompahgre Formation. (All photographs by Donald Baars.)

Plate 2. Silverton, at the southwestern edge of the Silverton caldera, a Tertiary volcanic vent. Note the glacial hanging valley, upper right.

Plate 4. The broad U-shaped valley of Mineral Creek was carved by alpine glaciers during Pleistocene time. The peak in the distance is a glacially sculpted horn in the Silverton Range.

Plate 5. Pigeon Peak, at the west end of the Needle Mountains, is a magnificent horn of Precambrian granite, carved by glaciers.

Plate 6. The summit of Mount Sneffels from the high shoulder of Kismet. The rocks are the San Juan Volcanics of Tertiary age.

Plate 7. Snowdon Peak. This mountain consists of nearly vertical quartzite beds of the Precambrian Uncompahgre Formation.

Plate 8. Arrow and Vestal peaks in the Grenadier Range rising to nearly 14,000 feet. These mountains consist of quartzite and slate that were highly folded and thrust-faulted in Precambrian time. The two sheer faces on the cliffs, especially Wham Ridge, left, are both bedding surfaces of quartzite rising skyward on a thrust fault.

Plate 9. Engineer Mountain and Coal Bank Pass from the shoulder of Snowdon Peak. The Coal Bank Pass fault lies along the gray cliff at the lower left and offsets Pennsylvanian age rocks, right center, upward to the high shoulder of Engineer Mountain.

Plate 10. A train of the Durango & Silverton Narrow-Gauge Railroad climbs into the Animas River Canyon just beyond Rockwood. The river has carved the deep canyon from metamorphic rocks of the Precambrian Twilight Gneiss.

Plate 11. Ice Lake Basin and the Silverton Range, glacially excavated from rocks of the San Juan Volcanics. The sharp peak at right is the Golden Horn.

Plate 12. Gladstone Peak from the west flank of Wilson Peak. The rocks in this San Miguel Range are Tertiary igneous stocks intruded into highly altered rocks (hornfels) of the Mancos Shale of late Cretaceous age.

Plate 13. Wilson Peak, a horn eroded from an igneous stock in the
San Miguel Range. Note the active rock glaciers emanating from
the glacial cirques.

Plate 14. Mount Sneffels and the Sneffels Range from the northwest, dominating the view from near Ridgeway to Dallas Divide.

Plate 15. The Ophir Needles tower above New Ophir near Lizard Head Pass south of Telluride. The rock is an intrusive igneous stock of Tertiary age.

Plate 16. Mount Abrams towers above Uncompahgre Canyon
south of Ouray. Rocks in the canyon walls are in the Precambrian
Uncompahgre Formation, capped directly by Tertiary volcanic
rocks.

Enter Man

T
First Invaders

he Four Corners region may have been occupied by primitive, nomadic people perhaps as early as 11,000–12,000 years ago, but evidence of their passing is sketchy at best. These earliest inhabitants hunted the woolly mammoth about the time the last Pleistocene glaciers retreated up the valleys of the San Juan Mountains. Perhaps they explored the partially glaciated mountains in search of game. The nomads were still wandering hunters and food gatherers in about 6,000 B.C. They gradually began to settle down and raise food crops, and by A.D. 200 were well established horticulturists, known as the Anasazi ("ancient ones") to the Navajos.

Anasazi culture is well documented by their artifacts. Pottery, baskets, stone tools, and ruins of pit houses and cliff dwellings are scattered profusely about the plateaus and mesa tops of the region. Mesa Verde, between Durango and Cortez, was the cultural capitol, but archeological sites have been found in the foothills of the San Juan Mountains. A popular mummified woman, known as Esther, formerly displayed in the Mesa Verde museum, was found, along with other important artifacts, in Falls Creek Valley near Durango. By A.D. 750 the

Anasazi were cultivating corn, squash, and beans and living in relatively large mesa-top villages of greater than 150 rooms.

During the 1100s and 1200s the Anasazi moved from their surface dwellings to better protection in coves underlying and within the huge sandstone cliffs that typify the country. They built single dwellings and condominium-like complexes of stone in every well-protected nook and cranny in the myriad cliffs, apparently for protection from marauding bands of nomadic Indians–probably the early Utes and Navajos. Sometime after A.D. 1250 they abandoned their elaborate cliff dwellings and left the region, most heading south to the Rio Grande Valley in New Mexico and to the Hopi villages of Black Mesa in northern Arizona. There is evidence of a 30-year drought beginning in A.D. 1270; the drought and overpopulation probably were contributing factors to the mass exodus, and pressure from nomadic peoples may have prompted the withdrawal. For whatever reason or reasons, the Anasazi had completely departed the Four Corners region by A.D. 1300.

Indians We Know

Ute Indians and their close relatives the Paiutes (pronounced "pie!-yoot"), arrived in the region by A.D. 1200. The Navajos are known to have occupied northern New Mexico by A.D. 1500, but their whereabouts prior to that time is a mystery. Navajo mythology indicates that there had been communication with the Anasazi, placing them in the region by A.D. 1300. Navajo legend sheds little light on their origins, indicating that the ancestral Dineh ("the people" in Navajo) arrived through an opening in the earth somewhere near present-day Silverton in the high San Juan Mountains, with no prior ancestral roots in this world. However, linguistics studies suggest an athapaskan origin in westernmost Canada at some time in the distant past. The exploring Spaniards documented their presence in 1626 and 1630, naming them for their agricultural lifestyle (*navaju* is believed to have meant "area of cultivated lands").

The various Indian tribes of the Four Corners region occupied lands separated largely by the physical geography. Paiutes stayed largely west of the Colorado River, Utes dominated mountainous regions of eastern Utah and western Colorado north of the San Juan River, and Old Navajoland was primarily south of the San Juan River in north-central New Mexico. There was always regional overlap, and intertribal raiding parties were active between recognized territories into the 1890s. Although the Utes dominated the San Juan Mountains, Navajo hunters frequented the region for its plentiful game. Each of the tribes had reputations of being hostile, both to neighboring tribes and later to Spaniards, Mexicans, and invading Americans in turn. Skirmishes with both the Utes and Navajos hampered prospectors in the San Juan Mountains as late as the 1890s. It is probable that Indians climbed several of the high peaks prior to the arrival of the prospectors. Rosebrough reported that there was "direct evidence" that Indians had extended hunting expeditions "at least to an elevation of 13,000 feet" on Uncompahgre Peak. Although the Navajos split from their cousins, the Apaches, early in history to become agriculturalists and pastoral peoples, they obtained their prized horses, sheep, and goats from Spanish settlers by raids on outposts in the Rio Grande Valley.

Spaniards

The Spaniards settled in the Rio Grande Valley near the mouth of the Chama River in 1598. They founded Santa Fe in 1610 and made it the capital of New Mexico. From Santa Fe, exploring expeditions were launched into and across southwestern Colorado. One of these expeditions was led by Don Juan Maria de Rivera in 1765 into the San Juan Mountains to the Uncompahgre Plateau, the Uncompahgre River, and the Gunnison River. He is believed to have found silver in the La Plata Mountains, and named the range accordingly (*La Plata* is Spanish for "silver"). Another expedition was led by Francisco Atanasio Dominguez and Francisco Silvestre Velez de Escalante in 1776. They traveled across the La Platas and northwestward in search of an overland route to California that would bypass the Indian territories in

Arizona. These Spanish explorers named many of the geographic features in the area, including the San Juan Mountains. It wasn't until 1830–31 that William Wolfskill and George C. Yount established the Old Spanish Trail that generally followed the route of the Spanish Fathers.

Army

United States Army units came into this area during the Mexican War in 1846 and in following years in efforts to deal with the Indians. Among the men were Major William Gilpin, Colonel J.C. Frémont, and Captain J.W. Gunnison. Ute Indians especially plagued the early mountain men and prospectors in the San Juan and La Plata mountains. The army had little success in protecting the civilians, as both Ute and Navajo warriors were difficult to locate in their lofty homelands.

Geologists

Early geological work in southwestern Colorado was conducted by J.J. Newberry in 1859, Lt. E.H. Ruffner and J.J. Stevenson in 1873. The Hayden Survey, led by A.D. Wilson and including Frederick M. Endlich, Franklin Rhoda, and William Henry Holmes, not only mapped the San Juan Mountains, but accomplished first ascents on many of the major peaks, including Stewart Peak in 1873, and Handies Peak, Sunshine Peak, Mount Sneffels, and Mount Wilson in 1874 in the course of establishing survey stations. According to Rhoda, members of the Hayden Survey climbed Uncompahgre Peak, the highest summit in the San Juans, on August 8, 1874, with little difficulty. They "were terribly taken aback, however, when, at an elevation of over 13,000 feet, a she grizzly, with her two cubs, came rushing past them from the top of the peak." Wheeler Survey parties were also active in the area and recorded first ascents on Redcloud Peak and Rio Grande Pyramid during the 1874 and 1875 field seasons. Members of the Wheeler Survey also climbed Uncompahgre Peak in 1874, and reported "a large cinnamon bear and her cub . . . sportively tumbling and rolling from the summit." Such episodes may have attracted Indian hunting parties to the peak. The first geologic and topographic map of Colorado was made by the Hayden Survey in 1877.

Whitman Cross

Reconnaissance surveys by the Hayden and Wheeler teams attracted further mapping efforts by United States Geological Survey geologists in the 1890s. Parties led by Whitman Cross made detailed geologic and topographic maps of the entire western San Juan Mountains that are still regarded as masterpieces today. They traveled the rugged mountains by pack train and on foot, missing few details of the complex geology. Indians, accustomed to invasion by prospectors and believing the geologists insane for crawling around looking at the rocks, were of little concern.

"Charles Whitman Cross was born at Amherst, Massachusetts, September 1, 1854. From Amherst he received the B.S. degree in 1875 and the Sc.D. at Leipzig [Gottingen] in 1880. He returned to the United States in 1880, joined with the U.S. Geological Survey, and for some years was stationed in Denver. He was a member of that organization until his retirement in 1925." (From a biographical memoir in the *Year Book of The American Philosophical Society,* 1949, by Esper S. Larsen). Cross also received an honorary D.Sc. degree from Amherst College in 1925.

Soon after being appointed to the USGS for an annual salary of about $3,400, Cross was mapping in the Colorado mountains. His first USGS folio on the Pikes Peak area was published in 1894. His seven folios on the San Juan Mountains were published between 1899 and 1910. The final summary of this work, written with E.S. Larsen, Jr., was eventually published as Professional Paper 258 in 1952.

Cross was aided in the field by numerous younger geologists and topographic engineers, among them A.C. Spencer, Ernest Howe, J.D. Irving, R.D. George, G.W. Stose, Albert Johannsen, L.F. Noble, Esper S. Larsen, Jr., and C.S. Ross. In the biographical memoir written after Cross's death, Larsen stated:

"The field parties of Cross were training schools for young geologists and it was a privilege to be a member of his party. He, a great field geologist, was friendly, sympathetic, generous, and patient with young men and he was ready to listen patiently to their ideas and to keep them straight in their thinking. He had a great influence on the younger men and was a truly great and inspiring teacher." This may have been written in extreme politeness, for Whitman Cross II later recounted in a personal letter his grandfather's "strong, driving personality," his "occassional [sic] brashness and dogmatic approach to life," and ". . . the cast of people who often looked on dealing with him as a major confrontation! . . . He was generally thought of as an uncompromising man with strong ideas and persuasive tendencies."

Whatever his personality, there is no doubt he was a great field geologist. His published maps and descriptions of the San Juan Mountains were meticulous in detail and accuracy, especially for the conditions under which he worked. Again from the Larsen memoir: "The San Juan Mountains are a rugged group with many peaks rising to altitudes of 14,000 feet, and while Cross was working in the mountains there were few roads or inhabitants. The field work with Cross was done with horses or on foot and camp was moved by pack-train [on muleback]. The country was wild and difficult to traverse but Cross believed in living comfortably and his camp outfit was one of the best in the West. He had had much experience with such camps and he knew that he must have superior camp men and a comfortable, adequate outfit. He selected camp sites with care and usually had a beautiful view and pleasant surroundings."

Indeed, Charles Whitman Cross (he never liked the name Charles and dropped it later in his life, to be known as Whitman Cross) concentrated so heavily on this work that his only son, Richard Stevens Cross, was not born until the elder Cross was 40 years old. Unlike Whitman, Richard had no interest in geology and " . . . tried to study psychology in college, but was pulled out of the University of Virginia by CWC when he would not study the hard sciences! He never recovered from this trauma . . ." according to Whitman Cross II.

Cross continued his studies of igneous rocks and, with Joseph P. Iddings, Louis V. Pirsson, and Henry S. Washington (known collectively as the Four Horsemen), published the classic *Quantitative Classification of Igneous Rocks* in 1902. He also published *Lavas of Hawaii and their Relations* in 1915.

Among numerous professional accomplishments, Whitman Cross was a member of the National Research Council, the National Academy of Sciences, American Philosophical Society, and was elected president of the prestigious Geological Society of America in 1918.

H.S. Yoder, Jr., wrote in the *Dictionary of Scientific Biography, Supplement IV* (1974): "Retirement in 1925 did not mark the end of Cross's scientific career; his systematic methods were transferred with equal vigor to the cultivation of roses. He developed new varieties, some of which became available commercially. The outstanding varieties include 'Chevy Chase,' 'Mrs. Whitman Cross,' and 'Hon. Lady Lindsay.'" His garden in Chevy Chase, Maryland, reportedly contained two thousand rose bushes; he received the gold medal of the Potomac Rose Society in 1941.

Whitman Cross II wrote: "Physically . . . Whitman Cross entered Amherst College and fell under the wing of Isaac Porter(?) who took this '90-pound' weakling to the gymnasium and built him into a true dynamo of energy that carried him throughout his life even to be seen in his great strength at age 93, which I can remember." Whitman Cross died on April 20, 1949, near Washington, D.C., at the age of 94 years.

Whitman Cross served the geological profession well. Maps in his seven folios on the San Juan Mountains are as accurate and detailed as any; we are still trying to interpret some of the idiosyncracies in the rocks that he mapped nearly a century ago. In hindsight, we see that he made a couple of errors in judgement, but without his work the story told in this book could not have been written today. Unfortunately these folios are long since out-of-print, but the giant topographic–quadrangle-size publications can be found in almost any university library, lying somewhere in a dark corner because they are too big to shelve. They are fascinating to anyone with an interest in geology, geography, or the San Juan Mountains; they are historically the most significant geological publications on the San Juan Mountains to date.

Prospectors

Early prospectors were responsible for attracting settlers to the region by broadcasting overstated reports of their finds. One of the first of these was Charles Baker, who went into the San Juans near Silverton in search of placer gold in 1860. He pioneered a route from Del Norte, southeast of the mountains, up the Rio Grande, across Stony Pass, and into Baker's Park, now known as Silverton. Although that was the hard way to get there, a road was completed along the route in 1875, following the discovery of ore near Summitville in 1870.

Meanwhile, Baker and a party of prospectors were panning for gold where the Animas River exits its deep, rugged canyon onto the broad Animas Valley at what is now called Baker's Bridge. They were plagued by belligerent Ute Indians, who finally chased the prospectors from the mountains into the desert country of southern Utah. There, in a running gun battle, the Utes caught up and killed Baker. Two survivors, George White and a friend, fled northward back across the San Juan River, or so they thought, with the Indians in hot pursuit. They reached a river White believed to be the Grand (Colorado), hastily built a raft of driftwood, and escaped down the river. The raft flipped in the first rapid, and the companion was reportedly drowned. White tied himself to the raft and, although it was flipped repeatedly in the savage river, he emerged from the Grand Canyon ten days later, near death from starvation and exposure. He later claimed to be the first man to run the river through Grand Canyon, a feat later disproved. White had been hopelessly lost and apparently had actually run the Virgin River. It was left for Major John Wesley Powell to be the first to run the Grand Canyon, in 1869.

Prospecting in the Silverton area was very active in the 1870s following the Summitville discovery, attracting many prospectors from California and Nevada mines. About 1870, the town of Del Norte was founded, and it became the main gateway to the mines of the San Juan Mountains. Most of the towns of the area were settled between 1870 and 1890. The many discoveries in the region, among them the remarkable deposits found at Red Mountain and Ironton in 1881, caused the "Rush to the San Juans." Transportation over Stony Pass was seasonal at best and ore shipments were minimal until the Denver and Rio Grande Railroad Company completed the narrow-gauge line from Durango up the Animas River to Silverton in 1882.

Animas City was haphazardly established at the mouth of the Animas Valley in the early 1870s as the region's trading center. The Denver and Rio Grande Railroad wanted to use Animas City as their terminal to supply miners in the San Juan and La Plata mountains and from which to ship ore. A difference of opinion over the terms of the deal prompted the railroad to establish its own town, Durango, a couple of miles to the south in September of 1880. It is not clear how the town was named, but it was known as Durango almost from the beginning. *Durango* means "village" in Spanish, but there is a Durango in Mexico and an older Durango in Spain, either of which may be the namesake. By mid-October, 1880, John Porter had begun construction of the smelter at the south edge of Durango and "by mid-November, Durango's business district had seven hotels and restaurants, two blacksmith shops, two bakeries, eleven saloons, dance halls, meat markets, general stores, and a variety of other (largely unmentionable) businesses." In two short months, Durango had become the "City of the Silver San Juan" (Duane A. Smith, *Rocky Mountain Boom Town: A History of Durango*, University of New Mexico Press 1980). With the completion of the spectacular rail line to Silverton two years later, Durango prospered, and other villages such as Animas City, Parrot City, and Hermosa dwindled into insignificance.

Durango again became the center of activity in the mid-1950s when major accumulations of oil and gas were found in the Aneth Field of southeastern Utah. The Aneth discovery was made by Texaco in 1956 following minor discoveries of oil at nearby Desert Creek by Shell Oil Company in 1954. Exploration activity was feverish, with numerous oil companies, both

An abandoned mining operation in La Plata Canyon, west of
Durango and north of Hesperus in the La Plata Mountains.

large and small, establishing exploration offices in Durango; oil
service companies settled in Farmington, New Mexico, and
Cortez. Despite quiet disapproval by the city fathers, some 350
petroleum geologists, geophysicists, and their families bol-
stered the local population and economy of Durango in the late
1950s and early 1960s. The oil boom was accompanied by a
frantic search for uranium in the Four Corners region in the
1950s, with some exploration activity also centered in Durango.
The old smelter on the south edge of Durango was converted
into a uranium concentration mill, a high-profile boost to the
town's economy and, secondarily, its olfactory makeup. Although the search for oil and uranium was highly successful in
the Four Corners region, dwindling demands for the products
led to the gradual dissemination of Durango's professional population in the 1960s, and the town returned to domestic tran-
quility.

After several reversals of the economy in minerals, oil, and

Chapter Ten

ranching, Durango is again prospering, but currently the gold comes from the tourist industry. Excellent skiing at Purgatory attracts visitors during winter months, the narrow-gauge rail-road runs several trains to Silverton daily during the summer, and excellent hunting draws many Texans to the mountains in the autumn. Even during the spring months when a ruthless economy rules, the students and faculty of Fort Lewis College contribute to the local economy. Whatever the appeal, Durango and the San Juan Mountains remain an economic oasis and a retirement community for the oil and uranium prospectors of yesteryear.

Part Two

Geologic Tour of the San Juan Mountains

Chapter 11

Mountaineering Geology

T he San Juan Mountains have been a mountaineering mecca for generations. They are high, they are rugged, and they are remote. At least 13 peaks rise to elevations above 14,000 feet. Some of the most interesting climbs are on the hundreds of peaks that attain elevations between 13,000 and 14,000 feet. Rocks in the several subranges vary from some of the hardest rock on earth to some of the rottenest. Very few have easy access by road. Expedition-style climbing is required to get to the bases of many of the best climbing mountains.

As in most mountainous terrain, the weather can be a serious problem. Winter snows usually make access to the higher peaks difficult until mid-June, and the first autumn snows usually occur in late August or at least by early September; it can snow on any given day of the year. Midsummer is the height of the thunderstorm season here, and they can be awesome. There is no thrill quite like climbing the north ridge of a fourteener, only to face a thunderstorm ascending the south ridge with claws bared. Hair stands on end, metal pack frames buzz, and adrenaline makes the descent faster than expected. A climb must be planned so that one is well down from the summit and high ridges by noon on a summer day, not an easy task on many of these mountains.

Clothing and camping equipment must be capable of protecting against unexpected storms and cold. It is also wise to carry an emergency supply of food in the event of being stranded temporarily by the weather or an injury. Of course, never climb alone in these very remote ranges. It is easy to sprain an ankle, break a leg, or wrench a back coming down a seemingly harmless talus slope, and rockfalls can be devastating. Sturdy climbing boots are a must on these mountains, which are blanketed with extensive talus almost everywhere above timberline (timberline varies between 11,000 and 11,500 feet).

Whether one is collecting fourteeners or simply loves to climb mountains, the San Juans are the place to go for excitement. A little understanding of basic geology adds another dimension to the enjoyment of this fabulous area.

This chapter is not intended to be a guide to climbing routes, but presents instead a discussion of the geology of the various subranges. Approaches and routes are given for key peaks for orientation to geology that is described. For details on routes for specific climbs, especially on technical climbs, *The San Juan Mountains: A Climbing and Hiking Guide,* by Robert F. Rosebrough (Cordillera Press, Inc.), is recommended.

Engineer Mountain

Probably the best warm-up climb in the San Juan Mountains is Engineer Mountain, a 12,968-foot summit that rises above and west of Coal Bank Pass north of Durango. Don't be mislead—there are three Engineer Mountains on maps of the San Juans, and there is an Engineer Pass that is many miles distant from this peak. This Engineer Mountain is a lone peak that is obvious for several miles along the Durango-Silverton highway (U.S. Highway 550) near Purgatory Ski Area.

The best approach is to drive to Coal Bank Pass and climb the grassy slope above and west of the pass to an obvious notch along the Coal Bank fault. There is a small, marshy pond just beyond the notch, and a short distance farther, a trail leading up

Engineer Mountain from near Little Molas Lake. Rocks forming the lower cliff at left and in the foreground are on the Hermosa Group of Pennsylvanian age; the base of the high peak is on the Permian Cutler Formation; and the double crown of the engineer's hat forming the summit is eroded from an intrusive igneous sill of Tertiary age.

(southwest) toward the peak. A more scenic lower route is to climb along the edge of the high, gray cliff that forms the lower shoulder of the mountain. The alternating beds of limestone, sandstone, and shale constitute the Hermosa Group of Pennsylvanian age. The topmost limestone that forms the prominent high shoulder (the Desert Creek Stage of the Four Corners area) contains huge crinoid stalks with individual segments as large as silver dollars.

From the high bench midway up the mountain, the final route is obviously the northeast ridge. Red rocks in the lower slopes and cliffs of the summit peak are in the Cutler Formation of Permian age. Three hundred feet of limestone conglomerate derived from the north side of the Coal Bank fault in lower Permian time occur at the base of the formation. Light gray rocks that constitute the upper mountain and summit are remnants of an intrusive igneous sill of Tertiary age. Exposure to height is minimal, occurring about midway up the high, gray ridge, affording a good near-vertical view of a classic rock glacier at the foot of the west face. The northeastern of the two summits is the highest.

A panorama of southwest Colorado greets the summit party. The long, U-shaped valley to the south is the Animas Valley, with the high La Plata Range bordering the valley to the west (right). Graysill, with its light gray cap of the same sill as the summit of Engineer Mountain, is in the middle distance to the southwest. Grizzly Peak lies to the west, capped by extrusive igneous rocks of the San Juan Volcanic Series (Tertiary age). To the north is the high country near Molas Lake, part of the Silverton West Range, with Grand Turk and Sultan mountains west of the lake, also capped by extrusive igneous rocks, and Snowdon Peak carved from Precambrian quartzite to the northeast. The expanse of high ranges to the east beyond Coal Bank Pass and Potato Hill (Spud Hill), are the West Needles Range that, like Potato Hill, consists of older Precambrian metamorphic rocks. The Needle Mountains of massive Precambrian Eolus Granite and the Grenadiers, consisting of upturned layers of Precambrian quartzite, lie beyond to the east.

Snowdon Peak

Another good warm-up climb is Snowdon Peak (13,077 feet), just east of Molas Pass. A dirt road heading east from U.S. Highway 550 just south of Molas Pass goes to Andrews Lake at the foot of the climb. The lake lies on limestones and sandstones of the Hermosa Group (Pennsylvanian age) that are faulted against Precambrian rocks midway between the lake and the high peak. The nearly vertical, west-facing wall of Snowdon is a dip-slope, or bedding surface, of quartzite layers of the late Precambrian Uncompahgre Formation. Quartzites of the high peak, in turn, have been thrust-faulted in late Precambrian time on top of older metamorphic rocks.

After crossing the small dam, a trail leads to the left (north)

Snowdon Peak from Little Molas Lake. The lake is on beds of the
Pennsylvanian Hermosa Group, but the peak is comprised of
quartzite of the Precambrian Uncompahgre Formation. The steep
smooth cliff on Snowdon is formed on bedding surfaces of the
quartzite, standing nearly on edge. The Snowdon fault separates the
two rock units, running across the view near timberline.

Mountaineering Geology   *105* and winds up a steep hillside of Hermosa sedimentary rocks. It first tops out at a small pond at the base of the west wall of Snowdon Peak, and then crosses upturned beds of Cambrian conglomerate against the Precambrian fault. From here, take any direct route to the prominent low col on the skyline and follow the easy south ridge, marred only by a short rock scramble across a small notch, to the summit ridge of Precambrian quartzite.

There is an unexcelled view to the east across the Animas River canyon of the Needle Mountains Range of late Precambrian Eolus Granite (1.46 billion years old), and the Grenadier Range of somewhat older Precambrian Uncompahgre quartzite. The West Needle Range of older Precambrian Twilight Gneiss is to the south, and Engineer Mountain is the prominent peak to the southwest. From here it is obvious how Engineer Mountain got its name. The upper peak has the appearance of an old-fashioned engineer's hat, and the edge of the lower Hermosa cliffs has the profile of a man's face. Grand Turk and Sultan peaks to the west display a well-developed angular unconformity between red rocks of the Cutler Formation upturned against the overlying flat-bedded Telluride Conglomerate and extrusive igneous rocks of the San Juan Volcanic Series that form the skyline. This unconformity resulted from the initial uplift, followed by erosion, of the San Juan dome. The view north is toward Molas Lake and Silverton.

The west face of Snowdon is a nearly vertical bedding surface on quartzite layers that dip to the west. A Precambrian-age fault cuts the north edge of the summit ridge, and quartzite beds along the north ridge, across the fault, dip steeply toward the northeast. A descent of the north ridge constitutes sliding down steeply inclined quartzite beds toward the Animas River canyon, making this route more difficult and tricky than the south ridge.

Twilight

Twilight Peak (13,075 feet) dominates the West Needles Range south of Snowdon and east of Engineer Mountain. The approach trail for Twilight Peak is the same as the trail to the base of

The West Needle Mountains, with Twilight Peak the highest summit. The Animas River Canyon, lower right. Rocks in this range consist of a Precambrian metamorphic complex, the Twilight Gneiss, dated at about 1.78 billion years.

Snowdon. Stay on the main trail, crossing the large Precambrian fault, and traverse the ridge to the prominent saddle just north of the mountain, a distance of about five miles. Crater Lake just below the saddle on the east-west-trending Coal Bank fault is a good overnight camp. The near ridge is the easiest route, but there are many variations.

The West Needles Range and Twilight Peak are composed of older Precambrian basement rocks named the Twilight Gneiss (1.78 billion years old). There are many kinds of metamorphic rocks exposed in the range, but most are variations of gneiss and schist, cut by numerous granitic dikes. Gneiss is a rock that has undergone great changes due to intense heat and pressure, and consists of partially recrystallized quartz, feldspar, and other strange minerals that have been stretched and distorted into interesting patterns. It is usually hard rock in massive, steep faces, but becomes crumbly with intense weathering or fracturing. Schist is a very platy, brittle rock with abundant mica along cleavage surfaces, and is usually crumbly and unstable. Consequently, the rocks in the West Needles are not as good for rock climbing as granite or quartzite and should be treated with considerable respect.

The view from the summit of Twilight Peak is much like that of Snowdon. A deep cleft off the east face is the canyon of the Animas River, with Pigeon and Turret peaks in the Needles forming the opposite wall. Animas Valley, with its magnificent glaciated profile, leads toward Durango to the south, Engineer Mountain and the Purgatory Ski Area are to the west, and Snowdon Peak is the sharp ridge to the north.

The Needle Mountains

Most climbers use Chicago Basin as a base camp for climbs on any of the Needle Mountains. It can be approached by long back-packing trips via Vallecito Creek to the southeast or the Durango Reservoir from the south. The best approach, however, is to ride the Durango-Silverton Narrow-Gauge Railroad to Needleton, a regular stop, and then hike 7.5-miles up Needle Creek toward the east. The Needles consist of a series of horn-shaped peaks carved by Pleistocene glacial erosion from the late Precambrian Eolus Granite that was intruded into the basement about 1.46 billion years ago. Granite makes good, firm rock for climbing where steeper surfaces are not deeply weathered or highly fractured. Thus, the Needle Mountains Range is generally good for rock climbing.

The larger, more rounded peaks, Eolus (14,083 feet), Windom (14,082 feet), Sunlight (14,059 feet), and North Eolus (14,039 feet) constitute the "fourteeners" and occupy the southeastern highlands of the range. They provide routes of varying difficulty. Pigeon (13,972 feet) and Turret (13,835 feet) peaks to the west are the more difficult, both for their approaches and

The Needle Mountains in the core of the San Juan dome, with the Animas River Canyon at lower left. The dark gray rocks in the canyon walls are Twilight Gneiss, dated at about 1.78 billion years. The high mountains consist of the Eolus Granite dated at 1.46 billion years. The two sharp peaks on the far left are Pigeon and Turret; the more rounded summits on the right are Eolus, North Eolus, and Windom peaks, all rising above 14,000 feet.

summits. All are of granite, providing good rock except in fault zones.

Peaks of the northern Needle Mountains are usually approached by primitive trails up Ruby or Noname creeks from the Animas River Canyon, or Vallecito Creek on the east, a far more difficult route. It is a rugged, isolated group of 13,000-foot peaks of Eolus Granite. Because of their remoteness, these are probably the least visited peaks in the San Juan Mountains.

Mountaineering Geology

Grenadier Range

Peaks of the Grenadier Range form an impressive chain of quartzite sentinels north of the Needle Mountains. The summits consist of eroded, upturned layers of quartzite of Precambrian age that were thrust-faulted toward the south in Precambrian time into the most complex structural mess found anywhere in Colorado. Vertical wrench faults bound the overall fault block, all of which are in turn intruded by the Eolus Granite to the south. Numerous thrust faults in the range resulted from the large kink in the wrench-fault block. As the quartzite was forced to slide through the kink, localized forces jammed the rocks southward, away from the north-bounding wrench fault. The north faces of Vestal (Wham Ridge), Arrow, and related peaks are bedding planes that have been thrust skyward by these intense structural forces. The massif is a major fault block, or rock sliver, along the continental-scale wrench fault zone of late Precambrian age described in chapter 3. Removal of thousands of feet of overlying sedimentary rocks by erosion in Tertiary and Pleistocene time has exposed the intensely deformed fault block.

The best initial approach is from the Durango-Silverton Narrow-Gauge Railroad to the mouth of Elk Creek about ten miles south of Silverton. From there the easiest route to Arrow, Vestal, and the Trinity Peaks heads up Elk Creek by a primitive and difficult-to-follow trail. The eastern Grenadiers, such as Storm King Peak and Mount Silex, can be reached from the Vallecito Creek trail and bushwhacking up Trinity Creek. There are no established trails into the Grenadiers, and one may explore pristine routes to the peaks of choice. Although none of the summits quite reach 14,000 feet, they are among the most difficult and interesting of any major peaks in the Rocky Mountains. Wham Ridge, the north face of Vestal Peak, is perhaps the most famous. The rocks are very hard, consisting of quartzite that approaches two billion years in age, and high routes provide precarious exposure. These are the choicest rock climbs on major peaks anywhere in America.

Silverton Range West

The Silverton Range West lies, surprisingly, generally west of the town of Silverton. A dirt road heading west up South Fork of Mineral Creek off U.S. Highway 550 north of Silverton leads to the U.S. Forest Service campground. Golden Horn, a magnificent 13,780-foot-high matterhorn-shaped peak carved by glaciers from igneous rocks of the San Juan Volcanic Series, may be seen from the road junction. A trail from the north side of the campground winds up a mountainside of red Cutler Formation toward Ice Lake Basin above timberline. Ice Lake is a tarn nestled in rocks of the lower part of the volcanic series; the Golden Horn towers over the lake to the west. The climbing route is to the high saddle south of the peak through glacial debris and talus, then continues up the south ridge and relatively easy southeast face. The rock is composed of lava flows and solidified ash beds, and consequently is relatively soft and crumbly. Extreme caution should be exercised in climbing on such unstable and unfriendly rock.

Sneffels Range

Mount Sneffels (14,150 feet) is certainly the most prominent monarch of the San Juan Mountains, rising from green pastures near Ridgeway to its lofty summit in one grand escarpment. It dominates a massif of lesser crags carved from rocks of the San Juan Volcanic Series that lies southwest of Ridgeway, northwest of Ouray, and south of Telluride. The peaks of volcanic rocks ride piggyback on a high fault block of Precambrian quartzite, named the Sneffels block for the dominant mountain. Stony Mountain displays exposures of the quartzite basement. The north-bounding fault that controls the uplift runs directly south of Ouray through Box Canyon; the south-bounding fault flanks the valley at Telluride. This is the northern of two fault blocks that together are known as the San Luis Uplift. It is an exposed segment of a continental-scale wrench fault zone that extends from Oklahoma northwestward across Utah and perhaps beyond.

From Ouray, drive a half-mile south on U.S. Highway 550 to the Box Canyon junction and turn right. After crossing a narrow, but surprisingly deep canyon cut into the Precambrian quartzite, go straight on the steep, dirt road that leads to Yankee Boy Basin. The road first passes massive, gray cliffs of the Leadville Limestone of Mississippian age and crosses onto covered slopes of the Hermosa Group. A narrow, perched roadway crosses exposures of thick Telluride Conglomerate of early Tertiary age, before passing upward into dull gray rocks of the San Juan Volcanic Series. Keep right at the turnoff to the Camp Bird Mine, and drive to the end of the road. Climb along the right valley wall to the southeast couloir of Mount Sneffels, keeping right all the way. An adjacent peak, Kismet, dominates the view ahead and may distract the unwary climber.

From the summit, there is a grand view of other craggy peaks in the Sneffels Range, with Uncompahgre Peak and the Wetterhorn obvious toward the east. The Uncompahgre Plateau, a low, wooded topographic remnant of the late Paleozoic Uncompahgre Uplift, extends away to the north.

San Miguel Mountains

Mount Wilson, Gladstone Peak, Wilson Peak, and El Diente ("the tooth" in Spanish) form a cluster of fourteeners that stands alone, west of the main San Juan Mountains. Wilson Peak (14,017 feet) is the fine horn-shaped mountain that dominates the scenery between Telluride and Lizard Head Pass. Mount Wilson (14,246 feet) and El Diente (14,159 feet) guard the ends of a long rocky arete that extends westward from just south of Wilson and Gladstone peaks. The group represents the exhumed core of an igneous body that intruded rocks of the Mancos Shale in Tertiary time. Igneous rocks maintain the summits, while the highly baked, crumbly, black Mancos Shale dominates the approaches. The somewhat lower Lone Cone (12,613 feet), so obvious from the eastern Colorado Plateau, is an outlier of the range.

A campsite at the base of Wilson Peak is reached by driving 6.5 miles north from Placerville on Colorado 145 to the dirt road leading south into Big Bear Creek. It is a long, rough drive to Silver Pick Basin. The approach for all three summits is up the abandoned road toward the south, past a magnificent rock glacier and the abandoned Silver Pick mining camp, to a saddle between Wilson and Gladstone peaks.

Wilson Peak lies east of the saddle, and a direct route to its southwest ridge provides access to a rock scramble up the ridge. Like many climbs, Wilson Peak offers the disappointment of a false summit along the way. Spectacular views of the Mount Wilson-El Diente ridge dominate the scenery from the saddle to the summit, but Lizard Head, low to the southeast, teases the imagination.

To approach Mount Wilson, one must climb to the saddle and downclimb 600 feet into Navajo Basin below the west face of the mountain. A steep, rocky climb up various routes on the west face and the precarious summit ridge lead to the top. From there, the long, difficult arete of rocky snags and turrets (the Organ Pipes) leads tediously west toward El Diente at the far end. Because of the topographic layout of these peaks, Mount Wilson and El Diente are usually climbed together in a very long day. Unexcelled views of the Colorado Plateau country to the west dominate the scene from these summits.

Lizard Head (13,113 feet) guards Lizard Head Pass between Telluride and Rico on Colorado Highway 145. It is a tempting climb because of its outrageous appearance. Ormes's 1952 climbing guide to the Colorado Mountains describes the approach from the pass to the ridge directly west of the high snag. It then directs one to "Take photograph and go away." It is an erosional outlier eroded from rocks of the Silverton Volcanic series and consists of a spine of rotten igneous rock that is very dangerous; the climb is ranked as extremely difficult. It has been climbed several times since the first ascent in 1920, but the climb is not recommended.

Lake City West Group

The high country west of Lake City is dominated by three fourteeners—Handies, Redcloud, and Sunshine peaks. They are in the eastern San Juan Mountains, where the entire landscape is eroded from dull gray rocks of the San Juan Volcanic Series. A base camp centered among the three summits is reached by an often precarious dirt road up Lake Fork of the Gunnison River west of Lake City. It can also be reached from Silverton via a four-wheel-drive road up the Animas River and over Cinnamon Pass. Proximity of the summits of Redcloud and Sunlight dictate that both be climbed together. The climbs are up a crumbled, rounded mountainside, across an intervening high saddle, and down another steep scree and talus slope. Some also climb Handies Peak in the same day, but that requires great physical conditioning and an exceedingly long day. Handies is climbed by whatever route one fancies, up long, arduous talus slopes. It can also be climbed by a long traverse and talus scramble from near Cinnamon Pass on the Silverton side of the divide.

Scenery from all of these peaks constitutes a sea of gray summits of volcanic rocks extending to the horizon, or at least as far as Uncompahgre Peak to the northwest.

Top-o'-The San Juans

I first heard of the San Juan Mountains as a teenager learning to climb in the Pacific Northwest in the 1940s. Everett Darr, a noted local climber, encouraged Floyd Richardson and me to make the second ascent of St. Peter's Dome in the Columbia River Gorge (a first ascent for Darr's party) and our first ascent of Steins Pillar near Prineville, Oregon. In contrast to the overhanging walls of Steins Pillar, he related his experience of climbing the highest summit in the San Juans, Uncompahgre Peak. He had approached the base of the mountain by pack train, and decided to take the horses as far as possible. Darr said his horse couldn't make it up the last couple of hundred feet, but he had "put his name in the book [climbing register] anyway."

Uncompahgre Peak, with its neighbors the Wetterhorn and Matterhorn, rise above a high plateau east of Ouray and west of Lake City. It can be reached with equal discomfort from either Ouray or Silverton via Engineer Pass, or up Henson Creek from Lake City. From a camp between the three peaks, a well-trodden trail ascends the south ridge of Uncompahgre to the 14,309-foot summit. A rocky stretch of ten or fifteen feet at the very top excludes horses and motorcyclists (but not bears). Otherwise, the view is unexcelled. All of the fourteeners of the San Juans can be seen on a clear day, but a gutwrenching view down the north face into the headwaters of Cimarron Creek highlights the climb. Rotten volcanic rocks form the entire mountain.

The Wetterhorn, a peak that barely reaches 14,015 feet, is a much more interesting climb. Both the Wetterhorn and the smaller Matterhorn are classic examples of glacially sculptured horns. A rock scamper up the southeast ridge and an airy scramble over crumbly volcanic rock at the summit of the Wetterhorn brings one to an outstanding view of Uncompahgre Peak. It is well worth the trip.

San Juan Skyway

W e will begin our highway tour of the San Juan Mountains in Durango, Colorado. We will be driving north from Durango to Silverton via Coal Bank and Molas passes, on to Ouray via the Million Dollar Highway, then to Ridgeway. At Ridgeway we will turn left (west) to Placerville via Dallas Divide, and then south to Telluride. From Telluride we will head generally south again to Rico via Lizard Head Pass, then back to Durango through Dolores and Cortez. This is undoubtedly the finest long one-day, or easy two-day excursion one could possibly imagine. Depending on one's interests and pace, the 243-mile loop will take about eight hours to complete. This is mountain splendor at its best! In autumn, when the aspen leaves are turning their golden miracle, the trip is ecstasy. Although the route passes Mesa Verde National Park, one should not plan to include a visit to the spectacular ruins there on this loop drive unless an extra day is scheduled just for the park.

The route has recently been named the San Juan Skyway, a National Scenic Byway, by the U.S. Forest Service, and various types of markers, platforms, shelters, and rest stops are scheduled to be constructed along the route. These improvements will be in various stages of completion for several years. Only

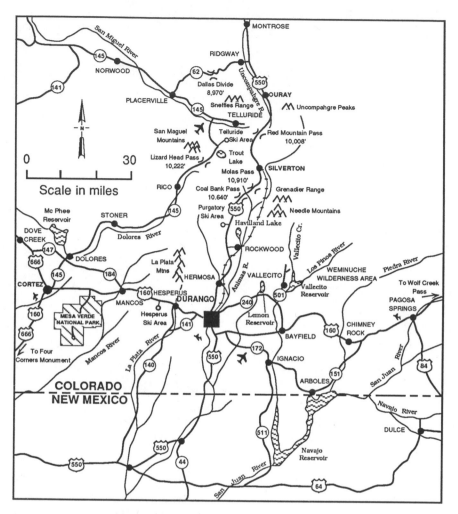

Fig. 14. The San Juan Skyway.

highway mile points will be mentioned here, as the exact locations and orientations of the Forest Service features are not yet
definite; only one exhibit was in place in June, 1991. Mile points
referred to are on the small, green Highway Department signs
located along the roads. However, these mileage markers are
often severely damaged by snowplows and have not been up-
dated to accommodate highway construction improvements.
Also, four different highways with different mileage starting
points comprise this loop drive, making use of the mileage

markers confusing and unreliable. Consequently, mileage has been measured from zero starting at the intersection of U.S. Highways 160 and 550 at the south edge of downtown Durango and tied to highway mile points where possible, noted in parentheses.

Durango

The San Juan Mountains were heavily glaciated during the past million years or so, as described in chapter 9. The Animas Valley north of Durango was shaped by one of the largest of the valley glaciers that relieved the southern half of the range of excess ice. The snouts of the several episodic glacial advances never seemed to get past the northern edge of Durango, as shown by relic local deposits in the form of lateral and terminal moraines. At the times of the various glacial epochs, the climate was such that the balance between ice flow and melt was reached at the 6,500–7,000 foot elevation at this precise geographic point. For each level of moraine an associated stream, or outwash terrace, developed. In addition, there are numerous terrace levels for which there are no recognized morainal deposits.

Downtown Durango lies in a restriction of the Animas Valley where the river has eroded its course across rather steeply dipping beds of Cretaceous age. The parallel terraces above the river that dictate the layout of the city are various outwash terraces below each terminus of a cycle of glaciation. The lowest terrace, where Main Street is located, represents outwash gravel from the latest period of glaciation, perhaps merely 15,000 years ago, known as the Pinedale glacial epoch. Two terminal moraines associated with this terrace flank both sides of 32nd Street on the north edge of town, lying in varying states of manmade destruction. The next higher and consequently older terraces accommodate 2nd and 3rd Avenues, formed from outwash from the small remnant morainal deposits that cap hills along Florida Road to the northeast of downtown Durango. This glacial event is known as the Bull Lake glacial epoch, dated at about 88,000–150,000 years ago.

College Hill, which is not really a classic hill but a high terrace

Aerial view of Durango northward toward the Animas River Valley. Animas City Mountain, capped by the Dakota Sandstone, is the low mountain left of center. Across the skyline, left to right, are Engineer Mountain, the West Needle Mountains, and the Needle Mountains. Fort Lewis College is situated on the high bench at lower right.

east of the main city, was shaped by the outwash from the oldest recognized glacial epoch in this area. The morainal deposits are still partially and poorly preserved along the ridge north of the golf course, hosting spectacular homesites and the old stone observation shelter; Fort Lewis College lies on the outwash terrace of this, the Durangoan glacial event, dated at about 250,00–330,000 years ago. It is important to remember that all of these dates are poorly constrained and highly generalized. A still higher and older terrace with no recognizable affiliated morainal deposits is Florida Mesa southeast of Durango in the vicinity of the Durango airport (La Plata Field). These terraces can be traced down the Animas River to Aztec, New Mexico, and farther westward along the San Juan River all the way to present-day Lake Powell. Thus the plan and configuration of Durango is necessarily arranged by glacially generated topography.

The best way to begin any geologically oriented tour of the Durango area and San Juan Mountains is to view the country from the old stone observation shelter atop the Durangoan moraine north of the golf course on College Hill. Travel eastward on 6th Street to its end and turn left up the winding, paved road to Fort Lewis College; this road can also be reached by turning north from the easternmost stop light on 8th Street. Take a left at the top of the hill for an overview of the four-year state college campus and outstanding views of downtown Durango and the La Plata Mountains to the west. Proceed northward and park at the north edge of the golf course and climb to the stone house, a short stroll.

The general view northward is of the broad Animas Valley with its U-shaped glacial profile, infilled to a flat bottom by glacially-fed lake deposits. The terminal glacial deposits are at your feet and directly below the escarpment in the low hills along Florida Road directly below and astride 32nd Street just beyond. At the head of the valley in the middle distance is Hermosa Mountain, and beyond and to the right are the West Needle Mountains in the core of the San Juan Mountains. The rocks exposed in the West Needles are the oldest in the San Juans, metamorphic rocks that date at nearly 1.8 billion years, lying near the crest of the structural dome. Between the West Needles and your vantage point, the steep valley walls are seen to be carved from colorful sedimentary rocks of Paleozoic and Mesozoic age that are dipping gently toward you, forming the south flank of the dome. The gray, layered rocks in Hermosa Mountain are the Pennsylvanian-age Hermosa Group; the red rocks of the middle Animas Valley are the Cutler Formation of probable Permian age. The red beds dipping below river level at the north edge of Durango represent the Dolores Formation of Triassic age, capped by two white cliffs of sandstone separated by a slope constituting the Entrada Sandstone, Wanakah Formation, and Junction Creek Sandstone of Jurassic age, in ascending order. Animas City Mountain, the cuesta-shaped ridge to the lower left, is capped by the Cretaceous Dakota Sandstone, supported by the greenish gray slopes of the latest Jurassic Morrison Formation.

To the west, the view is dominated by the La Plata Mountains. These consist of sedimentary rocks of late Paleozoic and Mesozoic age intruded by irregularly shaped masses of intrusive igneous rocks of Tertiary age. The gray foothills between the high peaks and Durango consist of the light-colored, cliff-forming Point Lookout Sandstone, the lower unit of the late Cretaceous Mesaverde Group. The low, dark gray slopes nestling the city are in the Mancos Shale, also of late Cretaceous age, which lies between the Dakota Sandstone capping Animas City Mountain and the ridge of Mesaverde rocks that form the southern boundary of the city. On southward, hogbacks of Pictured Cliffs and Farmington sandstones mark the boundary between the San Juan uplift and the Tertiary-age San Juan Basin to the south. The San Juan Basin is one of the largest sources of natural gas in the nation, producing gas from each of the sandstone formations visible around Durango and from the Hermosa Group visible to the north.

From this vantage point, one can view the entire geologic record of nearly two billion years of earth history. The sedimentary rock record here measures about 16,000 feet in thickness. If these rock layers were flat-lying, as they are in the San Juan Basin to the south, rather than dipping southward as they are here, one would have to drill a hole nearly three miles deep to see the entire section. Nowhere else is there known to be such a completely exposed, uninterrupted stratigraphic section.

Retrace your route to the junction of U.S. Highways 550 and 160 to set your trip odometer to zero. Turn right to the north city limits of Durango, where the mountain to the left is Animas City Mountain, capped by cliffs of the Dakota Sandstone of late Cretaceous age, with light-colored slopes below of the Morrison Formation of late Jurassic age. When leaving town, at about mile **4** (milepost 25), there is a good view to the right of the youngest pair of glacial moraines. The Animas River below the 32nd Street bridge is like a mountain stream, with a relatively straight, rocky course and fast-moving riffles. Above the bridge and the site of the low moraines, the river is sluggish and meanders considerably as it lazily makes its way across the flat lake sediments of the Animas Valley. At about this same point, two white sandstone cliffs rise from the valley floor to form the base of Animas City Mountain. The upper of these is the Junction Creek Sandstone and the lower is the Entrada Sandstone, separated by a slope of Wanakah Shale. A careful look at the top of the Entrada Sandstone reveals a dark gray bed of limestone, here only about two feet thick, that is the Pony Express Limestone (also called the Todilto Formation); all are Jurassic in age.

Durango to Coal Bank Pass

Turning the broad, rounded corner to the left and entering the more open valley, the red, high roadcuts reveal the Triassic Dolores Formation. The reddish brown, ledgy cliffs ahead forming either valley wall at about mile **4.7** (milepost 26), are in the Cutler Formation. These beds, here about 2,500 feet thick, are ancient stream deposits washed southward from the Uncompahgre Uplift in early Permian times. Near Trimble Lane, mile **8.7** (milepost 30), and ahead in Hermosa Mountain, the lower cliffs suddenly become gray; a disconformity sharply separates the red rocks of the Cutler above from the underlying interbedded, mostly marine limestones, sandstones, and shales of the Hermosa Group of middle Pennsylvanian age.

The prominent mountain ahead, Hermosa Mountain, is the type area for the Hermosa Group. The reddish brown cap of the mountain is Cutler overlying the gray, ledgy cliffs of the Honaker Trail Formation of the Hermosa Group. The lower, dark gray slopes are in the Paradox Formation of the Hermosa Group; a small exposure of white gypsum can be seen near the base of the slope near the lone A-frame house. This is the southeasternmost occurrence of evaporites at the margin of the Paradox Basin. The village of Hermosa is to the left; the skyline ridge on the right (east) is Missionary Ridge.

After the highway turns right and crosses the railroad track near mile **10.5** (milepost 32), the low, rounded hill sitting near the edge of the valley with a house and tall pine trees at the top is a *drumlin*, a type of moraine that forms beneath the glacial ice. Drumlins are usually found where broad, continental ice sheets have covered the land, and are rather rare in valleys formed by alpine glaciation.

The highway turns gradually northward again around the base of Hermosa Mountain, where lower ledgy cliffs of sandstone and thin interbeds of shale rise beneath the Paradox black shale slope. This is an unnamed, local deposit that has been interpreted to be an ancient delta, where sediments were carried down to the early Pennsylvanian sea by streams flowing from Precambrian rocks in the Grenadier fault block to the north. Although these deposits are about 800 feet thick here, they are not widespread and are not present in wells drilled near Durango and Hesperas to the south and west.

Massive, gray limestone cliffs rise to highway level ahead, representing the Leadville Formation of lower Mississippian age. Yellowish colored deposits at the base of the cliff on the left are spring-deposited travertine, the springs issuing from a small fault that crosses the valley at this point; note the small, faulted drape of the limestone across the valley.

For an interesting interlude, take the exit at mile **14.2** (after milepost 35) onto County Road 250, cross old U.S. 550, and drive straight ahead (middle fork of the road) to Baker's Bridge. The bridge crosses a deep gorge cut into the late Precambrian Bakers Bridge Granite by the Animas River at the site where Butch Cassidy and the Sundance Kid jumped off the cliff in the popular movie, landing miraculously in a small stream in California. This is the site of a gold prospecting camp established in 1861 by Charles Baker, later abandoned because they found little gold and the Ute Indians were a constant menace. Following the Civil War, Baker returned and was killed by Indians. A historic marker at the west bridge abutment commemorates these events.

The Bakers Bridge Granite is a coarsely crystalline, pink intrusive igneous rock that cooled and crystallized at about 1.42 billion years ago. It here forms the basement to the 16,000-foot-thick section of sedimentary rocks you have just seen in the Animas Valley. The rolling topography seen here above the gorge approximates the paleotopography upon which the sedimentary rocks were deposited. The low cliffs of quartzite seen just west of the bridge are in the McCracken Member of the Elbert Formation of late Devonian age. The quartzite exposures are at a lower elevation than the granite with no recognizable fault present, indicating that it only partially buried the ancient hill of granite. The Ignacio Formation of late Cambrian age that usually is present between the basement and the McCracken is missing, apparently by having lapped onto the granite hill and later being buried by the younger sediments.

Return to old U.S. 550 (now County Road 200) and turn right. The road follows the McCracken/granite contact for about 2.5 miles, with exposures of quartzite in the low cliffs on the left and granite on the right. Above the low quartzite cliffs is a covered slope of the upper Elbert Formation, with good exposures of the Ouray and Leadville Formations above in the next gray cliff. The mountain above is of the Hermosa Group. At the entrance to Shalona Lake on the Leroy English Estate and the railroad crossing, the lower Paleozoic rocks are well exposed in the cliffs ahead and to the right. About a quartermile north along the railroad tracks, just out of sight from the road, the nonconformity between the granite and the sedimentary rocks is well exposed. The top of the granite is a rolling surface that has been weathered to a red soil and later buried by the late Cambrian Ignacio Formation perhaps a little more than 500 million years ago. Low places on the weathered granite surface are here filled with conglomerate that consists of well-rounded quartzite pebbles and cobbles. The nearest known source of these quartzite cobbles is Coal Bank Pass more than 20 miles to the north. The conglomerate and granite hills are buried by arkosic sandstones and shales of the Cambrian Ignacio Formation, forming the low, ledgy slope and swale. Above the Ignacio swale is the prominent brown cliff of the McCracken Sandstone Member of the Elbert Formation. This McCracken cliff is the lowest rock unit visible from the road at the railroad crossing.

Above the McCracken cliff at the railroad tracks is a prominent tree-covered slope on the shaly upper member of the Elbert Formation of late Devonian age. Above this slope are gray cliffs of massive limestone and dolomite beds of the lower Ouray Limestone of latest Devonian to earliest Mississippian age, overlain at the prominent notch by the Leadville Formation of early Mississippian age. The lower, rather ledgy cliffs above the sharp notch are dolomite beds that were deposited on extensive tidal flats that covered the entire Four Corners area and beyond in earliest Mississippian time. Then the sea withdrew to the Cordilleran seaway to the west for a brief period, when weathering formed an erosion surface that extends from here westward through Grand Canyon, where it marks the middle of the Redwall Limestone. Above this the massive, gray limestone cliffs are in the upper Leadville Formation, which is here very fossiliferous and locally oolitic. Rockwood Quarry, which is partially visible from the railroad crossing, was used to obtain very pure lime ($CaCO3$) for the ore smelting process in Durango in the early 1900s.

Proceed up old U.S. 550 a short distance to the junction with new U.S. 550 and turn right toward Silverton. The old road has here crossed sharply upward through the lower Paleozoic rocks to the disconformity at the top of the Leadville Limestone. In late Mississippian and early Pennsylvanian time, the Leadville Formation was exposed to weathering and a thick, red (lateritic) soil zone formed. The red soil zone (paleosol) was named the Molas Formation for its exposures at Molas Lake. Because the formation is very soft and easily eroded, its outcrop forms a broad bench between the more resistant Leadville below and Hermosa above. The highway follows this prominent bench from here to Cascade Creek beyond the Purgatory Ski Area. Occasional roadcuts reveal the nature of this deeply weathered surface, which consists of irregularly shaped, deeply weathered limestone residuum enclosed in a matrix of red claystone.

The Hermosa Cliffs, made up of the Hermosa Group of Pennsylvanian age, are to the left (west) from here to Coal Bank Pass. The group consists of cyclically interbedded marine fossiliferous limestones and shales, interspersed with sandstones laid down by streams flowing from the ancient Uncompahgre Uplift to the north. Only the lower half of Pennsylvanian time is represented here, as the upper beds were eroded from the San

The Hermosa Cliffs, left, and Lime Creek Canyon. The bedrock of
the valley is the Precambrian Twilight Gneiss, named for the
highest peak in the West Needle Mountains, visible at upper right;
rocks in the cliffs are Paleozoic. Note the strong asymmetry of the
valley, formed by the Animas glacier as it skidded sideways down
the dip of the very resistant Precambrian metamorphic rock surface

Juan dome prior to deposition of the Cutler Formation. This
entire section, above the basal Pinkerton Trail Formation, is
age-equivalent to the Paradox salt beds in the Paradox Basin to
the west and northwest.

The highway follows an asymmetrical valley from Baker's
Bridge to Coal Bank Pass, with abundant evidence of glacial
erosion, such as polished and scoured surfaces on the bedrock.
The strata are here dipping gently to the southwest and west,
and gravity caused the glaciers to slip down this dip-slope
during their erosional processes, crowding the ice against the
Hermosa Cliffs along the more resistant surface of the Precambrian and Mississippian rocks to form this unusual cross-
section of the valley. The ice was nearly 2,000 feet thick here,

reaching nearly to the top of the Hermosa Cliffs during its heyday.

The first road to the right leads to Rockwood, originally a railroad station at the entrance to the deep Animas River Gorge. The entrance to Tamarron Resort is the next exit. Fresh road-cuts along the left (west) side of the highway opposite the entrance to Tamarron are the best place to see the Pinkerton Trail Formation, the basal unit in the Hermosa Group. The road to the right at the top of the long grade leads to Haviland Lake, a beautiful place for a picnic stop. A short distance (two miles) farther is the entrance to Electra Lake, formerly known as the Ignacio Reservoir, the site of an older private community of vacation cabins, and the Tacoma hydroelectric plant. The reservoir is fed by Elbert Creek, along which are the type sections of the Ignacio and Elbert formations. About 1.5 miles farther on U.S. 550 is the Needles Country Square, where there is a magnificent rare view of the Needle Mountains to the right, from here dominated by Pigeon Peak (13,972 feet). The range was eroded from the Eolus Granite, an intrusive igneous stock that was emplaced about 1.46 billion years ago.

The mountain dominating the view ahead from here to Coal Bank Pass is Engineer Mountain, reaching an elevation of 12,968 feet. The gray cap rock is intrusive igneous rock, emplaced within the Cutler Formation, probably in Tertiary time. The reddish-brown rocks in the base of the upper peak represent the lower Cutler Formation; the lower, gray, layered cliffs are the Hermosa Group. The lower, more rounded mountain to the right (east) is Potato Hill, also called Spud Hill, and the jagged, higher peaks farther to the right are in the West Needle Range, the highest being Twilight Peak at 13,158 feet. Both Spud Hill and the West Needles consist of Precambrian basement metamorphic rocks, the Twilight Gneiss, that date at about 1.78 billion years old.

The entrance to the Purgatory Ski Area is on the left about four miles past the Needles Country Square. A ride up the high chairlift provides a spectacular view of the surrounding mountains and access to some fine skiing during the snow season. Just beyond Purgatory is a view of Grizzly Peak (to the left at the

Engineer Mountain, from a location near the Purgatory Ski Area. The lower cliffs are sedimentary rocks of the Pennsylvanian Hermosa Group, and the lower slopes of the upper peak are on the Permian Cutler Formation. The mountain is capped by a sill of light-colored intrusive igneous rocks of Tertiary age.

sign pointing out Engineer Mountain ahead), capped by Tertiary volcanic rocks, at the head of Cascade Creek. A short distance beyond, at the sharp hairpin curve, the highway crosses Cascade Creek. Take the first dirt road immediately beyond the hairpin curve and drive to the first cable guardrail for a view of a beautiful little waterfall below, but watch your step. The massive cliffs are in the Leadville-Ouray Formations of late Devonian to early Mississippian age. Nearly the entire section is dolomite and displays all the signs of having been deposited on a tidal flat. Rocks visible in the creek bed below the waterfall are in the upper Devonian Elbert Formation. The entire section down to the Precambrian basement is exposed farther down along the creek bed, and some good-sized trout can be found

Lower Paleozoic section between Cascade Creek and Coal Bank Pass along U.S. Highway 550. The slope at lower right is the Cambrian Ignacio Formation in its shaly facies. Bedding surfaces here contain numerous trails and resting marks of trilobites, but no fossil trilobites have been found. The cliffs at left are in the McCracken Sandstone Member of the Elbert Formation.

there, too. Here the Cambrian Ignacio Quartzite is nearly double its normal thickness and contains considerably more shale than elsewhere.

The dirt road is the old wagon road to Silverton and continues ahead into Lime Creek and rejoins the highway between Coal Bank and Molas passes. Although it passes through a beautiful, cliffy canyon, the road is not for the faint-hearted, as the rough, rocky trail enters the canyon perched high atop a cliff with no room for guard rails. For flatlanders, the paved highway is highly recommended.

Cascade Creek to Coal Bank Pass

The highway first passes through roadcuts in the Leadville-Ouray Formations. Looking back across to the other mountainside, large fractures in the basement rock are clearly marked by aspen trees; these are quite vivid in the autumn when the aspen leaves turn a bright yellow. Just past the cliffy roadcuts, the dug-up ground on the left is the site of a nearly buried diatreme, the neck of an ancient explosive volcano containing kimberlite, the host rock elsewhere of diamonds. On the right-hand bend at mile **32.1** (milepost 53) (past the barrier gates that close the road when it is blocked by avalanches), the highway again passes roadcuts in the dark red, ancient soil zone of the Molas Formation. This is a good place for a geologic stop at a wide turnout on the right. Be very careful of highway traffic here.

Above the right-hand lane of the highway, the deeply weathered and highly altered top of the Leadville Formation contains large, irregularly-shaped residual blebs of light gray, very fossiliferous limestone in the red soil zone. The fossils are mostly the bead-shaped segments of crinoid stalks that nearly comprise the entire rock composition. Crinoids are stalked, usually attached to the seafloor, almost flower-like animals that belong to the phylum Echinodermata. Even the heads (calices, or crowns) of the crinoids, usually frustratingly rare, have been found here. The red Molas Formation is well exposed in the roadcuts along the left-hand lane, but here a gray, igneous sill has intruded the middle of the formation. A highly baked and bleached contact zone between the intruded red beds and the intruder igneous sill is readily apparent. Although these igneous rocks have not been radiometrically dated, they were probably emplaced in Tertiary time.

For the next 1.25 miles, the roadcuts on the left provide the best exposures of the lower Paleozoic section. The first sheer cliffs are in the Leadville-Ouray Formations, which grade downward stratigraphically into the shaly upper Elbert Formation that contains abundant evidence of a tidal flat origin, including rare salt casts. The cliffs at the end of the continuous roadcuts are in the McCracken Sandstone Member of the Elbert Formation. A covered slope follows, but the next nearby reddish and greenish roadcut is a rare exposure of the late Cambrian Ignacio Formation in its shaly facies. It was here that the first datable oboloid brachiopods were found (small, about 0.25-inch, nearly round, black or rarely white, phosphatic shells). Here the softer,

A fossil oboloid brachiopod found in the Cambrian Ignacio
Formation in Cascade Creek. The fossil is about one-half inch in
diameter.

shaly beds rest directly on the Precambrian Twilight Gneiss, the oldest rock (1.78 billion years) in the San Juan Mountains.

The dark gray, massive rock from here to Coal Bank Pass is the Twilight Gneiss forming the basement. Natural surfaces along the way are highly scoured and polished by glacial abrasion. Stop in the large parking area at Coal Bank Pass at mile **35.8**, elevation 10,640 feet. This area provides the culmination of a very important geologic story.

Behind you and perhaps a hundred yards back on the opposite (south) side of the highway is an exposure of a soft, dark red rock that looks much like the Molas Formation, but here it is a highly weathered soil zone at the top of the Twilight Gneiss; the time of weathering was no doubt late Precambrian through early Cambrian. Walk down along the right-hand (west) side of the head of the gully, another 100 yards or so, where cliffy exposures of conglomerate are resting on nearly vertically inclined foliated (appearing to be bedded, but probably not) schist of Precambrian age. Cobbles and boulders in the conglomerate are rounded and consist entirely of quartzite of the Uncompahgre Formation (still ahead). This conglomerate can be walked-out and seen to change first to sandstone and then to the shaly beds of the Ignacio Formation at the last stop where the brachiopods were found. The Ignacio Formation is of late Cambrian age. The conglomerate is here overlain by a few feet of bedded sandstone and the nearly white quartzite of the McCracken Member of the Elbert Formation of Devonian age; again it can be walked-out to the last exposure down the highway. The bench and slope above the McCracken is the upper member of the Elbert that is considerably thinner than at the last roadcut; the cliff atop this slope is a much-thinned dolomite of the Ouray Formation, here seen to have sedimentary structures suggesting a tidal-flat origin.

Walk back to the highway along this bench, and rocks of the upper Elbert are exposed in the roadcuts at the pass. The Ouray dolomites just beyond have here been thinned to about 15 feet, down from the 100 or so feet at the last roadcut. Recross the highway and take the low path to the right (east) below the restroom structure. The first low exposures are again conglomerate, consisting of very large, angular blocks of quartzite, up to two feet in diameter, resting directly on the Twilight Gneiss; the conglomerate is here only about five or six feet thick. The nearly white quartzite of the McCracken Member that the rest-room sits on rests directly on the conglomerate, but a few yards to the west toward the highway leaving the pass, the conglomerate pinches out and the McCracken Member sits directly on the gneiss.

The very steep slope of the mountainside north of the pass is along the Coal Bank Pass fault. You are standing on the high, up-thrown block on the top of the Precambrian gneiss looking straight across the near gully at rocks that occur high in the Hermosa Group, the same rocks that form the Hermosa Cliffs and the base of Engineer Mountain above the pass. There has been a nearly 700foot vertical displacement along the fault. The fault extends through the notch above the pass, along the steep slope toward the east to cross through the notch north of the base of Twilight Peak.

Drive on around the sharp turn leaving the pass and stop at the first turnout for a beautiful view of the West Needle Mountains to the east and Snowdon Peak to the north. North of the fault, near the base of the steep slope of Spud Hill and Coal Bank Pass, there are a couple of lakes and a sheep pen far below on the down-thrown side of the fault. Exposures in that area tell quite a different story. There the Precambrian basement is steeply up-turned quartzite and slate beds of the Uncompahgre Formation, instead of the Twilight Gneiss. There are no Ignacio or Mc-Cracken beds present; the upper Elbert, with a one-cobble-thick basal conglomerate, rests directly on the Precambrian quartzites. And the Ouray there is a limestone with marine fossils, rather than a dolomite deposited on tidal flats. What could all of these changes be trying to tell us?

Interpretation

The segments of rock described above are depicted in cross-section in Figure 15. It clearly demonstrates that the Precambrian rock type changes dramatically at the fault, with older gneiss to the south and younger quartzite to the north. It also shows that the conglomerates, consisting of only quartzite boulders, are concentrated near the fault, having come only a short distance from the source of the boulders on the north side of the fault. This means that the north side was already higher topographically than the south when the Ignacio was deposited, and the Precambrian quartzite was already juxtaposed with the gneiss along the fault in late Cambrian time. The fact that the Cambrian section thins markedly toward the fault suggests that a slope was present at the time of deposition, and this is confirmed by the progressively coarser sediments as the fault is approached; the sea was shallower near the fault and deepened rapidly away from the structure.

That the McCracken Member of the Devonian Elbert Formation abuts the fault and does not cross it indicates that the higher topography remained present to the north after some 125 million years, and the fault was probably rejuvenated during, or shortly before, the late Devonian. However, the Ouray Formation consists of tidal-flat deposits south of the fault, but contains open marine fossils to the north, indicating that movement along the fault at that time, and the resulting topography, was reversed. Before Pennsylvanian time, the Leadville Formation was stripped from the top of the structure as fault movement was again reversed. (See the generalized discussion of this important structure in chapter 4.)

Prior to the detailed study of these rock sections by Paul D. See and myself in the late 1950s, it was generally believed that this was just another Laramide (late Cretaceous) fault. However, the salient features you have just seen require that the fault had undergone recurrent movement several times long before Cretaceous time. This realization completely revolutionized the structural history of the Colorado Plateau and southern Rocky Mountains regions. The subsequent realization that these are continental-scale wrench faults that were repeatedly rejuvenated completely reformed our understanding of the structural style of the western United States.

At about mile **37.4**, past Coal Bank Pass, there is a turn in the highway to the left with good exposures of Hermosa in road-

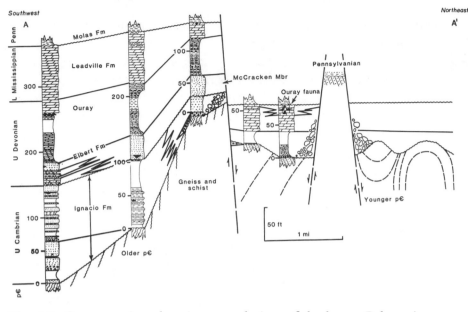

Fig. 15. Cross-section showing correlation of the lower Paleozoic rocks from Cascade Creek on the left through the Coal Bank Hill roadcuts to the Coal Bank Pass area and fault. Rocks shown at the right of the fault on the downthrown side are near the small lakes and the sheep pen along Coal Creek, where the upper Elbert Formation lies directly on upturned Precambrian quartzite. Note that all of the formations thin and change character near the fault.

cuts to the left and a parking turnout on the right. An angular unconformity, where the beds below were tilted and eroded before the overlying bed was deposited, may be seen about midway up the exposure. Sighting along this surface and the roadcut reveals that the angularity of the lower bed becomes more acute toward the north. At the end of this long roadcut, about 0.1 mile farther, the entire set of beds, including the unconformity, are abruptly turned on end by drag on the Snowdon fault. This tells us that the last movement on the fault was after deposition of the Hermosa limestones and sandstones, but the very local angular unconformity, increasing in angularity toward the fault, indicates that there had been previous movement actually during deposition of the Hermosa strata. Earlier movement, pre-Pennsylvanian, is demonstrated here by Her-

Chapter Twelve

mosa rocks resting directly on Precambrian quartzite, below the highway on the right.

Less than a mile ahead, at mile **38.1**, is the Lime Creek overlook and marker explaining that the reforested Lime Creek burn across the valley ahead was the site of a forest fire in 1879 that devastated 26,000 acres. Replanted trees, a project begun in 1911, have still not reached maturity. The rock strata beneath the burn lie in a syncline, or down-fold, created by drag along the Snowdon fault, which may be seen in the sharp gully to the right, and an igneous intrusion which forms the gray hills to the left. Isolated exposures of Cambrian(?) quartzite-boulder conglomerate occur along the Snowdon fault, in the gray gully to the right of the burn, from here to the base of the high cliffs of Snowdon Peak. The dirt road visible below is the Lime Creek Road heading back toward Cascade Creek, joining U.S. Highway 550 just ahead.

About 1.5 miles farther along the highway is the contact of the igneous intrusive body with the baked sedimentary rocks of the Hermosa Group. After the road makes a hairpin turn, crossing Lime Creek (elevation 10,000 feet), the gray roadcuts are intrusive igneous rocks, probably Tertiary in age, technically called a sanidine trachyte porphery. After the next broad, left curve of the highway, a small waterfall on the left marks another contact zone of igneous and sedimentary rocks. The shape of the igneous body is very irregular, rather resembling a branching cactus. Thus, it has been called a "cactolith," technically defined as a "quasihorizontal chonolith composed of anastomosing ductoliths whose distal ends curl like a harpolith, thin like a sphenolith, or bulge discordantly like an akmolith or ethmolith." Like all sciences, geology has its own technical vocabulary.

From the waterfall to Molas Pass, the highway is on the Hermosa Group. Notice that the sedimentary rocks consist of sharply interlayered marine limestones and stream-deposited sandstones. The shoreline and sea level must have fluctuated back and forth here several times during middle Pennsylvanian time. At milepost 63, the dirt road to the right leads to Andrews Lake at the base of Snowdon Peak.

Molas Pass, elevation 10,910 feet, at mile **43.1** (milepost 64), is worth a stop to fully appreciate the magnificent scenery. Molas Lake lies below and to the northeast. Grand Turk and Sultan mountains to the left are capped by the gray San Juan Volcanics, which overlies the early Tertiary Telluride Conglomerate in the upper steep cliffs. Notice that the gray Tertiary deposits overlie red strata with angular discordance; the Paleozoic rocks are dipping toward the west at a steeper angle than the rocks above. The unconformity marks the initial uplift of the San Juan dome in latest Cretaceous to earliest Tertiary time. The red rocks here beneath the erosion surface are in the Cutler Formation, overlying the Pennsylvanian Hermosa Group.

The deep canyon just to the right (east) of Molas Lake is the Animas River canyon, up which the Durango–Silverton Narrow–Gauge Railroad runs. The long ridge of peaks across the canyon toward the northeast are capped by Tertiary San Juan Volcanics and Telluride Conglomerate, overlying lower Paleozoic strata and the deep gorge composed of Precambrian Twilight Gneiss. Snowdon Peak, towering above Molas Pass to the right (east) consists of nearly vertical beds of quartzite of the younger Precambrian Uncompahgre Formation faulted into juxtaposition with Paleozoic strata. Major faults separating these various geologic terrains lie near the base of the Snowdon Peak escarpment, and others cross the canyon near Molas Lake.

This area was heavily glaciated during the Pleistocene Ice Ages. Scallop-shaped glacial cirques line the higher ridges, especially well seen across the Animas Canyon, and hanging valleys terminate each cirque where the smaller glaciers joined the major Animas glacier. The smoothed, rolling slopes to the north of the pass have been polished by the ice; Snowdon Peak was a nunatak, or island, surrounded by glacial ice.

Molas Pass to Molas Lake offers a magnificent view of the Grenadier Range to the east. These peaks, which rise to nearly 14,000 feet, consist of upthrusted sheets of Precambrian quartzite and slate, having been thrust-faulted southward from the north-bounding faults of the Grenadier fault block some 1.7–1.6 billion years ago. These peaks afford some of the best rock climbs in southwestern Colorado (see chapter 11). The dirt road to the left 0.2 miles beyond the pass leads to Little Molas Lake, a beautiful picnic and fishing spot. About 0.2 miles farther is a U.S. Forest Service San Juan Skyway display on the left, explaining the Lime Creek Burn, but using somewhat different dates than at the previous roadside marker. There is a magnificent view of Snowdon and the Grenadier Range in the opposite direction from the display.

Molas Lake (entrance road at mile **44.6**) occupies a natural shallow bowl carved by the glaciers at the top of the Mississippian Leadville Limestone. The obvious red shale bluffs immediately west and south of the lake are in the Molas Formation, named for this locality, an ancient lateritic soil zone that formed in late Mississippian to early Pennsylvanian time. Limestone hills surrounding the lake are called karst towers, as they are believed to be erosional remnants of Leadville Limestone that formed during the deep weathering that produced the Molas Formation. The rocks consist of very fossiliferous limestone, comprised primarily of fragments of crinoids, but many other kinds of fossil marine invertebrates may be found. This area has been the location for several movies, and remnants of a set for *Across the Wide Missouri* may be seen east of the lake, the view reminding one of Missouri country.

The main north-bounding fault on the Grenadier fault block trends westward from near Beartown, down Cunningham Gulch east of Animas Canyon, and up the west canyon wall to just east and down the mountainside from Molas Lake. The stratigraphic consequences are nearly identical, but a mirror image of, those of the Coal Bank Pass fault. The Ignacio Formation thickens northward from a quartzite-boulder conglomerate at the fault to sandstone and eventually to a shaly section toward Silverton. The McCracken Sandstone Member thickens northward from a pinchout near the fault to a shaly section; the Leadville-Ouray thickens and changes facies along the same line. These changes can be studied along either side of the Animas Canyon in three-dimensional detail from the Molas Lake area nearly to Silverton. Roadcuts along the highway enroute to Silverton provide the easiest access to the story.

Less than a mile from the north Molas Lake entrance road, the highway breaks over a hill and starts its steep descent into

Baker's Park and Silverton. At the start of the descent, the road is in the Leadville-Ouray limestones, but descends rapidly in the section through the upper Elbert shales to the white quartzite of the McCracken Member. Below this marker bed, the shaly section is in the Cambrian Ignacio Formation. Then, because the highway crosses small faults, the section is repeated several times, but it is clear that the massive Leadville Limestone is thicker each time it is crossed by the road. Finally, at mile **47.4**, with a good view of the town of Silverton below and a roadcut of limestone on both sides of the highway, an intrusive igneous rock (30-million-year-old quartz monzonite) cuts out the lower Paleozoic section. Numerous old dilapidated mines and tailings piles are visible in this zone of alteration and mineralization ringing the Silverton caldera.

At the road junction leading into Silverton, at mile **49.4**, a view down the Animas River to the right (south) reveals that the Animas Canyon was cut in at least two stages. The upper canyon walls form a U-shaped profile typical of glaciated valleys; into this was incised a river-cut, V-shaped canyon. Considering that glaciation ended between 15,000 and 10,000 years ago, the river has done a remarkable job of deepening the canyon into the hard, older Precambrian metamorphic rocks.

Silverton sits near the confluence of the Animas River and Mineral Creek, which collectively outline the southern and western margins, respectively, of the Silverton caldera. This is not a caldera in the strict sense, but instead it is the neck of an ancient volcano that first erupted about 30 million years ago. The forces generated during volcanic eruption created numerous faults that radiate from the neck, each having been invaded and filled with mineralized fluids to form veins. Mining from these veins produced large amounts of gold and silver, with some copper and lead, in the late 1800s and early 1900s. Today, gold is still being produced from the central part of the volcanic neck, but sporadically as prices fluctuate.

When the Denver and Rio Grande Railroad was completed into Silverton in July, 1882, the town became a bustling hub of mining activity. Later a railroad spur was built northward across Red Mountain Pass to Ironton, and another spur was built eastward up the Animas River to Eureka. A visit to Silverton, now designated a National Historic District, is a must for buffs of early mining history.

Silverton to Ouray via Red Mountain Pass

Leave Silverton on the street you entered, but turn right onto U.S. Highway 550. The highway follows Mineral Creek along the western margin of the Silverton caldera. Brightly colored red hillsides are the result of mineralization along the edge of the extrusive volcanic vent. Numerous abandoned mines and tailings dumps attest to the former wealth of the deposits, with some apparently new development in progress. The rust-colored streambeds result from iron mineralization of the waters flowing from mine adits, or entrances, in the region. A quick view west into the South Fork of Mineral Creek (road to campground at mile **51.4**) is of Hermosa (gray) and Cutler (red) sedimentary rocks, capped by volcanic rocks in the sharp summit of the Golden Horn in the Silverton Range. The dirt road to the left at mile **54.3** is a four-wheel-drive shortcut to Ophir. Then the climb up to Red Mountain Pass beyond the hairpin curve gives magnificent views of the U-shaped glaciated valley of Mineral Creek and the horn of Sultan Peak to the right of the valley. The dirt road to the left (west) at Red Mountain Pass at mile **59.2** is a shortcut to Telluride, but a four-wheel-drive vehicle and a total lack of fear are necessary.

Just after crossing Red Mountain Pass (elevation 11,075 feet), the Idarado Mining Company entrance to Treasury Tunnel is visible below. From this entrance at mile **61.0**, approximately 100,000 feet of drifts and 37,000 feet of crosscuts are accessible, connecting this entrance to the Mill Level tunnel six miles distant to the northwest high above Telluride. Several northwest-trending veins have been mined for gold, silver, lead, copper, and zinc since the late 1800s along the southwestern margin of the Sneffels basement fault block. Red Mountain, colored by mineralization of the northwestern margin of the Silverton caldera, hosts numerous abandoned mines of the Red Mountain Mining District.

Numerous switchbacks north of the pass lead to Ironton Park, one more classic U-shaped, formerly glaciated valley that is another abandoned mining district. In the high gullies to the right (east), rocks of the Devonian Ouray Limestone rest directly on upturned beds of the Precambrian Uncompahgre Formation on the Sneffels fault block.

At Ironton (mile **66.1**) the highway drops abruptly into the canyon of Uncompahgre Creek, a sharp, stream-eroded canyon cut below the glaciated open valley of Ironton Park. Near mile **66.8** (milepost 88) is a memorial plaque for the Reverend R.F. Miller and his two daughters, who were killed by an avalanche 0.2 miles farther along the highway at the present site of the snowshed. This stretch of highway is known as the Million Dollar Highway. No one seems to know the exact origin of that name, but various versions indicate that it was applied because the road cost more than a million dollars to build, or that it was originally surfaced with a million dollars' worth of gold ore, or several variations on these themes. The road was originally built by Otto Mears as a toll road in the late 1800s at a cost of $40,000, which was a huge sum at that time. It was finally paved and guardrails installed in the mid-1950s.

Rocks in the canyon walls are near-vertical beds of quartzite and slate of the Precambrian Uncompahgre Formation, named for these exposures along Uncompahgre Creek. For the first mile, the rocks are seen to be dipping steeply toward Ironton Park (south) and bedding surfaces display large-scale ripple marks. Then at 0.8 miles beyond the memorial marker, the beds roll over in a very tight anticlinal fold and dip just as steeply toward Ouray (north). An abandoned mine high on the west canyon wall marks the very abrupt turnover. High on the canyon walls is an ancient erosional surface upon which rests drab, gray volcanic ash deposits of the Tertiary-age Silverton Volcanic Series. Shortly past this point, at mile **68.4**, a dirt road to the right is a four-wheel-drive road that leads to Engineer Pass and Lake City to the east or Silverton to the south.

Bear Creek Falls, at mile **69.4**, is an interesting stop. The falls are rather spectacular, dropping more than 200 feet from beneath the highway bridge. Rocks in the canyon walls are highly scoured and polished by glaciation, and the undulatory surface opposite the falls across Uncompahgre Creek are huge ripple marks on the Precambrian bedding surface. For the next mile, rocks of Devonian and Mississippian age appear between the gray Tertiary ash deposits and the near-vertical Precambrian quartzites. They overlie the Precambrian rocks on a classic angular unconformity and underlie the ash deposits beneath the Tertiary unconformity. The short but vertical cliff low on the left (west) at mile **70.7** is a crinoidal sediment mound (some would call it a reef) in the Mississippian Leadville Limestone, perched on the high side of the Ouray fault.

Switchbacks leading down to the town of Ouray (here pronounced "your!-ray") beginning at mile **71.0** descend across the Ouray fault that may be seen to pass beneath the Box Canyon sign on the cliff at the left. This fault zone is the north-bounding margin of the Sneffels basement fault block. The view to the right (east) into The Amphitheater includes an angular unconformity high in the red cliffs, where the Triassic Dolores Formation overlies and truncates the Permian Cutler Formation, indicating that the fault block was rising after the Cutler was deposited and prior to deposition of the Dolores Formation. At mile **71.0** the dirt road to the right toward the Amphitheater Campground traverses a huge landslide deposit.

A short side trip to the left at mile **71.7** to Box Canyon city park is well worth the small entrance fee. After walking across the low hill at the gate, the vertical rock wall on the left is the plane of the Ouray fault. To get a feel for the vertical displacement along the fault, the Box Canyon sign high and to the left sits at the top of the Mississippian Leadville Limestone on the upthrown block; the light-colored ledge at creek level below on the right is also the top of the Leadville on the downthrown side; the red shale just above creek level is the Molas Formation. The rocks into which the spectacular falls of Box Canyon are cut are in the Precambrian Uncompahgre Formation; the rocks in the mountainside to the right are of the Pennsylvanian-age Hermosa Group. Those who feel the need for some good exercise may climb the stairs to the top of Box Canyon for a view of a magnificent angular unconformity. Here beds of the Precambrian Uncompahgre Formation are standing nearly vertical, overlain by nearly flat-lying dolomites of the Devonian Elbert Formation. The Precambrian quartzites were folded and eroded to a smooth plane before the Devonian sediments were deposited. There are no Cambrian or McCracken sandstones present here on the high side of the fault, as was the case along the Coal Bank Pass fault; however, these rocks are present in mines on the downthrown side.

The hot springs of Ouray come from deep beneath the surface, where the water is heated before rising to the surface along the fault zone. The Uncompahgre River, into which the hot springs eventually flow, was named for the Ute Indian word meaning "water that never freezes" or some variation on that translation. It is also said to mean "water rushing over red rocks."

Ouray, another National Historic District and sometimes called the Switzerland of America, was named for Chief Ouray, "The Arrow," a peacemaker between the Ute Tribe and white settlers. The town was first settled by prospectors in July, 1875, after the discovery of gold and incorporated in October, 1876. It is the center of the Uncompahgre, or Ouray, Mining District from which mainly gold, but also silver and lead, was mined most recently from mines in Yankee Boy Basin west of town.

Driving north from Ouray on U.S. Highway 550, the canyon walls consist of first the gray-colored cliffs of the Hermosa Group, but then the massive, reddish arkosic sandstones and conglomerates of the Cutler Formation, here of late Pennsylvanian to early Permian age. The course sands and gravel were deposited by streams along the mountain front of the Uncompahgre Uplift, which lies only a few miles to the north and east of this area. The formation was named for exposures along Cutler Creek about 2.5 miles north of Ouray. A pleasant picnic area (Rotary Park) at mile **73.9** is a good place to examine the Cutler Formation near its type location.

Softer slopes and ledges above and north of the Cutler outcrops are in Mesozoic strata, similar to those just north of Durango, dipping generally northward away from the San Juan dome. A vertical, dark-colored igneous dike cuts these strata at the Cutler-Dolores Formation contact, visible on the right at mile **78.1**. From here the west canyon wall to the left is capped by the Cretaceous Dakota Sandstone, a covered slope of the Jurassic Morrison Formation, and light-colored cliffs of the Entrada Sandstone lying on the largely covered red slopes of the Triassic Dolores Formation. More massive, brownish red cliffs of the Cutler Formation form the lower canyon walls. The top of the Cutler Formation occurs at mile **78.7** (milepost 100). A fault that drops the Mancos Shale down against the Dolores Formation may be seen to the left from mile **81.3**.

The village of Ridgeway lies in the Cretaceous Mancos Shale. Turn left toward Placerville on Colorado Highway 62 at mile **82.4**. Faults visible to the west form a graben (down-faulted block) in which the town sits. The fault north of town is the Ridgeway fault that offsets the Uncompahgre Uplift, now seen as the south end of the Uncompahgre Plateau, to the right (east).

Leaving Placerville, the road parallels the Ridgeway fault to the right on exposures of the Mancos Shale. The high mountains occasionally visible to the east (back) are the apparently square-topped Uncompahgre Peak, the highest point in the San Juan Mountains at an elevation of 14,286 feet, the small peak to the right is the Matterhorn at 13,589 feet, and behind is Wetterhorn Peak at 14,017 feet above sea level. The road ascends hills of Mancos Shale, capped by volcanic rocks beginning at mile **91**, to Dallas Divide (elevation 8,970 feet) at mile **93.2**, with spectacular views of Mount Sneffels (elevation 14,150 feet) to the left. Peaks of the Sneffels Range are capped by Tertiary volcanic rocks, but exposures of Precambrian quartzite occur well above the 12,000-foot level in the central, lower mountains in windows through the volcanics into the Precambrian Sneffels fault block.

Past Dallas Divide at mile **94.6** is an outcrop of the late Cretaceous Dakota Sandstone, overlying the late Jurassic Morrison Formation, which is well exposed at mile **95**. At the former site of the Dallas Divide Ski Area, the Dakota Sandstone caps the hill above the slope of Morrison Formation. Two-and-a-half miles past the ski area, the road crosses the Alder Creek fault, where the Entrada Sandstone and the overlying Pony

Express Limestone (both Jurassic in age) is faulted against the Morrison Formation. The Bilk Creek Sandstone overlies the Pony Express Limestone at about mile **97.9**, and the Entrada Sandstone is again well exposed near mile **99.4**. The highway again descends through the section, across exposures of the Pony Express and Entrada Sandstone to the top of the red Dolores Formation of Triassic age at mile **100.2**. There is a good view of the San Miguel Range at mile **101.7**. Then where the red rocks change downward to purplish red, cliff-forming arkosic sandstone at mile **104.4** is the top of the Permian Cutler Formation. At the intersection of Colorado Highways 62 and 145, at mile **105.7**, turn left toward Placerville and Telluride. The village of Placerville is nestled well down in the red rock country of the Cutler Formation.

The Placerville-to-Telluride highway follows the canyon of the San Miguel River, climbing gradually back up the stratigraphic section until it reaches the Dakota Sandstone again at the top of Keystone Hill at mile **118.0** (milepost 72) near the junction with the 3.3-mile highway spur into Telluride, known locally as Society Turn. In the late 1800s, the society people of Telluride would ride out of town this far on Sunday afternoons "to see, and be seen." Glacial deposits line the valley floor and walls in this area. Then, the rock strata are abruptly uplifted along two faults and an intervening monocline that are partially covered by glacial debris in the floor and lower walls of the valley. The town of Telluride lies near the top of the Cutler Formation in the well-developed, U-shaped glacial valley.

Rocks exposed in the north valley wall are nearly the entire Mesozoic section. In the large cliff to the left, the red beds are in the Dolores Formation; the thin, light brown, sandstone cliff above is the Entrada, overlain by the black Pony Express Limestone, capped by the thin-bedded Bilk Creek Sandstone Member of the Wanakah Formation; the upper member forming the wooded slope above. Below the main cliff, the Cutler Formation may be seen in scattered exposures in the trees. These westward-dipping, sedimentary rocks mark the western margin of the San Juan dome.

Telluride was the center of an 1890s mining district that

produced gold, silver, lead, and zinc from veins in the San Juan Volcanic series of middle Tertiary age. A network of veins extends from here to Red Mountain Pass. As the veins were being drilled out, pockets of oil would occasionally be encountered, making terrible messes in the mine. The vein system is believed to have developed along the south-bounding faults of the Sneffels basement fault block, and the oil probably seeped up through the fracture system from the Pennsylvanian Paradox Formation.

The tortuous track fighting its way up the steep head of the valley terminus east of town is known as Boomerang Road, leading up to the Alta mine in Turkey and Gold King basins. A lesser traveled trail, equally as tortuous, heading upward beyond the waterfalls and mine entrance is a shortcut back to Red Mountain Pass. This is strictly a four-wheel-drive trail, not for the faint-of-heart traveler.

Telluride is now a thriving ski resort in the winter, since the installation of lifts and clearing of trails began to the south of town in the 1970s, and is an art and festival center in the summer.

Telluride to Durango via Rico, Dolores, and Cortez

Return to Society Turn and go left (south) on Colorado 145 and cross the San Miguel River. The low ridge crossing the road ahead is one of several recessional moraines left by the Pleistocene glacier that formed Main Fork Valley in which Telluride is set. The valley was filled with glacial lake sediments that form the flat valley floor. Views ahead and to the right for the next few miles are of the San Miguel Range, consisting of the impressive pyramidal Wilson Peak (elevation 14,017 feet) and the long ridge extending from El Diente eastward to Mount Wilson (elevation 14,246 feet). The upland consists of an intrusive igneous stock of granogabbro intruded into the Mancos Shale and Dakota Sandstone, which were severely baked by the heat of the intrusion and stripped from the upland by subsequent erosion. Between this point and Sunshine Campground, topography in the lower regions is typical of hummocky landslide complexes, mantled by ground moraines. About two miles beyond the campground is a view of Lizard Head (elevation 13,113 feet), an erosional remnant of San Juan Tuff resting on the Telluride Conglomerate.

New Ophir, at mile **136.1**, was once a thriving mining town, along with the older town of Ophir about two miles to the east. Several mines in the vicinity produced gold, silver, lead, and zinc ores in considerable quantities. This was also the apex of the Ophir Loop on the line of the Galloping Goose operated by the Rio Grande Southern Railroad to the smelter at Durango. Remnants of the precariously perched roadbed may be seen both entering and leaving New Ophir. The road leading eastward to Ophir and beyond is a relatively tame four-wheel-drive trail to Silverton via Ophir Pass. The dull gray rocks in the vicinity of, and to the east of, New Ophir are a second stock of granogabbro, called the Ophir stock, somewhat smaller than the stock of the Wilson peaks region, and connected to the larger stock by a connecting-arm sill. These intrusive rocks are first seen at about mile **135.4**, and the southern intrusive contact between the Ophir stock and the highly baked Mancos Shale is near mile **137.8**.

A half-mile beyond New Ophir are the rugged Ophir Needles high above the road on the left. These ragged pinnacles have been carved haphazardly from rocks of the Ophir stock by erosion. At mile **139.0** is the road to Trout Lake and then to the left (east) is a good view of Trout Lake, nestled in a glacial-scoured valley, dammed and rimmed by landslide debris. The high mountain country beyond the lake is the Silverton Range carved from the Telluride Conglomerate and San Juan Tuff that have slumped promiscuously down steep slopes of the "greasy," highly baked Mancos Shale to nearly smother the lake basin.

Lizard Head Pass (actual elevation 10,222 feet) lies in exposures of the Mancos Shale at mile **141.0**. Lizard Head Station on the old Galloping Goose line is ahead and to the left. Spectacular Lizard Head, a most enticing sight to rock climbers, rises dramatically to the right (west) at mile **142.9**. However, see the precautionary comments in chapter 11 before attempting a climb on the rotten rock. It consists of San Juan Tuff overlying

Trout Lake in the San Juan Mountains north of Rico, Colorado, and Lizard Head Pass. These mountains of the Silverton Range were carved in Pleistocene time from extrusive igneous rocks of Tertiary age by the combined effects of glaciers and running water.

the Telluride Conglomerate. About two miles ahead there are spectacular views of both the San Miguel Mountains to the west and the main ranges of the San Juan Mountains to the east, including most peaks in the Silverton Range.

From here the road crosses downward through the Dakota Sandstone at mile **143.4** and begins its long descent through the stratigraphic section, into the heart of the Rico dome, at Rico. The strata may be seen to be dipping northward or northwestward, and the drainage system of the Dolores River, which the road follows, cuts directly into the structurally up-bowed dome. By mile **147.8** the road has cut down-section through the Mesozoic strata to the top of the typically exposed reddish brown cliffs of conglomerate and arkosic sandstone of the Cutler Formation. Then at about mile **150.8** the rocks become noticeably less red, and the rest of the drive into Rico is down through the Pennsylvanian-age Hermosa Group, here mostly consisting of sandstone with a few prominent beds of limestone.

Indeed, the mountain to the west of the road and the Dolores River, where the section is relatively well exposed, is named Sandstone Mountain.

This area is the type section for the Rico Formation, originally defined as a transitional unit. Although the actual relationships are not clear here, due to sketchy outcrops, the Hermosa-Cutler contact is regionally a disconformity and not transitional. See chapter 5 for a full discussion of this problem.

Rico (Spanish for "rich") lies at the structural crest of the Rico dome at mile **152.8**, where the Dolores River has cut the deepest into the Paleozoic rocks, perhaps to the base of the Pennsylvanian section. It is an old mining town, as made obvious by the many abandoned mines and waste dumps that scar the mountainsides in all quadrants. Some $26 million worth of silver and other base metals, mostly from the several mines on Newman Hill southeast of town, were produced from veins within limestones of the lower and middle parts of the Hermosa Group. Core drilling for exploration purposes has shown that the basement fault zone extends from Coal Bank Pass westward through the Rico dome, apparently influencing later mineralization, and greatly affecting rock thicknesses across the faults, as at Coal Bank Pass.

A great deal of pyrite was associated with the ores, and after mining ended for economical reasons in the 1950s, a sulfuric acid plant was constructed just north of town. The pyrite (iron sulfide, FeS_2) was converted to sulfuric acid (H_2SO_4) for use in leaching uranium ores in Uravan, Naturita, and Durango, Colorado; Monticello, Utah; and Shiprock, New Mexico. The acid plant was closed in 1964 following the collapse of the uranium industry, after doing considerable environmental damage around the plant; note the dead trees.

In the middle 1950s Rico was a company town, owned and operated by the Rico Argentine Mining Company, who worked the active mines and later the acid plant. The hotel, cafe, movie theater, and general store with the only gasoline pump were company owned and operated on credit, making it difficult for employees to be able to afford to move away. Many "owed their soles to the company store," as the song says.

As Rico sits at the crest of the Rico dome, the dip of the sedimentary rocks here changes from northwest to southwest south of town. Consequently, the Dolores River Valley, and the highway, now begins to climb up through the section, crossing into younger strata as they approach the town of Dolores. For about the next ten miles, the road crosses stratigraphically upward through the Pennsylvanian Hermosa Group and then enters the conspicuous red, cliffy sandstones and conglomerates of the Cutler Formation at mile **157**. In another four miles we can see the Cutler-Dolores Formation contact, and the road continues to climb stratigraphically up through rocks of Mesozoic age. At Stoner and across the valley from the former Stoner Ski Area, the massive reddish brown cliff is the Entrada Sandstone overlying the red beds of the Dolores Formation. The valley rimrock is the Dakota Sandstone from Stoner to Dolores.

Take the Dolores bypass at mile **188.8** to see the Galloping Goose railroad engine, used on the Durango-to-Ridgeway line. Dolores (Spanish for "pain" or "sorrow") sits in the Morrison Formation beneath massive cliffs of the Dakota Sandstone. After leaving Dolores, the highway crosses the Dolores River, now inundated by the reservoir of McPhee Dam, and climbs up through the Dakota Sandstone at mile **190.6**. The river here turns to the north, rather unexpectedly, finally flowing into the Colorado River several miles upstream from Moab, Utah.

The view from the high plain above the Dakota Sandstone at mile **192.0** is of the north scarp of Mesa Verde ("green table" in Spanish) ahead and Sleeping Ute Mountains to the right. From this area the profile of the Ute Mountains is said to resemble an Indian man lying on his back, with his arms folded across his chest and hair flowing outward toward the north, toes pointing skyward to the south. However, it looks like a reclining woman to me.

The Dakota Sandstone, late Cretaceous in age, underlies the broad plain that extends from the Dolores River Valley to Cortez and Sleeping Ute Mountain, south to Mesa Verde, and east to Mancos and the La Plata Mountains. These uplands are clearly visible along the route to Cortez and then east to Mancos. Turn left onto U.S. Highway 160 at the east edge of Cortez, mile **199.8**, toward Mancos and Durango.

Sleeping Ute Mountain is an igneous intrusive (laccolithic) range of about middle Tertiary age. Mesa Verde is capped by sandstones of the Mesaverde Group (late Cretaceous in age), overlying the dark gray slopes of the Mancos Shale. Most of the cliff dwellings in Mesa Verde National Park were built at the contact between the upper Cliffhouse Sandstone and the softer middle Menefee Formation; the lower unit of the group is the Point Lookout Sandstone, named for the prominent point that overlooks the park entrance. The Mancos Shale was named for exposures of the dark gray to black shale in Mancos River Valley, near the town of Mancos. *Mancos*, Spanish for "arm-less," was named by the old Spanish explorers probably because the river has no major tributaries in this area.

The La Plata Mountain Range, visible to the east, is another laccolithic igneous body, intruded into rocks of the Hermosa and younger formations. The name *La Plata,* the Spanish word for "silver," was given by the early Spanish explorers who found silver minerals in the mountains. Silver mines in the mountains have been periodically active for the past century. The highway between Mancos, mile **219.7**, and Durango climbs up into Mesaverde Group strata on the south shoulder of the range and provides good views of some of the igneous intrusive bodies; then it descends back down into the Mancos Shale at Durango, thus concluding the San Juan Skyway loop drive at mile **243**.

Chapter 13

The Silverton Railway

T
he completion of the railroad from Durango to Silverton in 1882 marked the end of a major engineering and construction ordeal and the opening of the high San Juan country. Prior to that time, supplies going into the mining districts around Silverton and the hauling of ore to smelters was by horse-drawn stages and wagons over tortuous and often precarious roads. The Denver and Rio Grande Western Railroad built and operated the line for a century and sold it to Charles Bradshaw, of Florida, in 1981. The original century-old, narrow-gauge steam engines, and the cars and depots, have been meticulously restored and serviced to maintain the flavor of the old mining days in southwest Colorado. The smallest of the three classes of engines used on the line weighs a quarter of a million pounds and uses six tons of coal and 6,000 gallons of water per trip. Sections of the tracks have been destroyed by the flooding Animas River on several occasions, making maintenance of the line an expensive and difficult proposition. A trip on The Silverton is a trip into the past, living history at its best.

Mileage figures used in this chapter refer to rail mileage markers, measured from Denver. Mileposts about eight inches square or metal signs standing six feet out of the ground are set

10–20 feet to the right of the track (when heading north) every mile along the way. Intermediate mileage points used here are approximations.

The railroad depot in Durango is at mile **451.5**. The heart of the 1880s Red Light District was at 11th Street, at mile **452**. It was here that the Hanging Gardens of Babylon and Nellie's were located; a block away on 10th Street were Bessie's, Jennie's, Mattie's, Variety Theater, Clipper, and Silver Bell. The railroad bridge over the Animas River is at mile **452.5**. One-and-one-half miles later the train crosses 32nd Street, which to the east (right) lies between the remains of two terminal moraines of the latest (Wisconsin) glacial stage. You will notice here that the river changes from a fast-moving mountain stream below to a sluggish meandering river above the moraines. The glacial deposits formed a natural dam behind which a glacial lake formed. The U-shaped glacial valley became filled with lake sediments that formed the flat present-day valley floor, in effect creating a local base level of erosion that changed the river's gradient.

At mile **456** the mountain at the left is Animas City Mountain capped by the Dakota Sandstone of late Cretaceous age. The railroad parallels U.S. Highway 550 from here to near Rockwood, at mile **469.1**, crossing exposures of the entire stratigraphic section going into progressively older rocks as the train travels northward. As the train enters the open Animas Valley, the brushcovered slopes beneath the Dakota caprock are on the Morrison Formation of late Jurassic age; then two prominent white sandstone cliffs appear, which represent the upper cliff of Junction Creek Sandstone and the lower Entrada Sandstone separated by a covered slope of the Wanakah Formation, all of Jurassic age. Beneath the Entrada are red exposures in large roadcuts of the Triassic Dolores Formation. Darker, brownish red cliff-and-slope topography of the Permian Cutler Formation are apparent by mile **459**. During times of flood on the Animas River, the tracks are often underwater along this stretch of the valley. The mountain that lies ahead at the end of the open valley is Hermosa Mountain, capped by the reddish basal Cutler Formation above gray cliffs and slopes of the Hermosa Group of

Pennsylvanian age; it is from these exposures that the formation, later made a group, received its name.

At mile **462.7** the train crosses U.S. Highway 550 at the village of Hermosa and begins its long climb into the high country. Immediately after crossing the highway the gray slopes on the left are black shales of the Paradox Formation of the Hermosa Group containing a nearly white bed of gypsum low in the slope. The low, rounded hill with a single house and tall pine trees rising above the valley floor to the right is a drumlin, a form of glacial moraine that forms beneath the glacial ice.

The train now climbs upward through thick local sandstones in the lower Hermosa Group, still progressing downward in the stratigraphic succession. At mile **466.4** there is a railroad cut in the red Molas Shale, and almost immediately the train begins crossing downward through massive gray cliffs of the Leadville and Ouray formations, breaking out onto a covered bench of the Devonian Elbert Formation at mile **468**. The tracks cross old U.S. Highway 550 at Shalona Lake, below to the right, with good exposures of the Cambrian through Mississippian rocks to the left culminating in Rockwood Quarry. The lower cliff on the left is the Devonian McCracken Member of the Elbert Formation. At mile **468.5** the tracks cross from the Cambrian Ignacio Formation onto Precambrian Bakers Bridge Granite, dated at 1.72 billion years; channeled topography and basal Cambrian quartzite boulder conglomerate marking the important nonconformity are exposed in railroad cuts to the left a quartermile past the crossing. From here to Rockwood the railroad climbs along the Elbert Creek drainage, with exposures of the Cambrian through Mississippian strata occasionally seen at the left.

Rockwood, once a lumber camp and stage stop at mile **469.1**, marks the gateway to Animas Canyon. Here the tracks enter exposures of the older Precambrian metamorphic rocks, akin to the Twilight Gneiss. These are the oldest rocks exposed in the San Juan Mountains, the final crystallization of the minerals dating at about 1.78 billion years ago. From here it is a long way down to the Animas River on the right side of the train. The cliff-hanger track here reportedly cost $100,000 per mile to lay, even in the early 1880s. At mile **471.3** is the Tacoma railroad trestle, and a mile later is the TacomaWestern Colorado Power Company plant. Water to run the power plant is siphoned and flumed from Cascade Creek into Electra Lake and then flumed to the plant at the top of the cliff. Ah Wilderness Dude Ranch is at mile **474**. The small park at mile **475.2** was the setting for the movies *Night Passage,* starring Jimmy Stewart, and *Denver and Rio Grande.* The tracks cross the Animas River again at mile **477.8**.

Excellent views open ahead of Pigeon Peak (13,972 feet) and Turret Peak (13,835 feet), with an occasional glimpse of Mount Eolus (14,083 feet) in the Needle Mountains between miles **479.5** and the Chicago Bridge at the lower end of Needleton Park at mile **481.5**. This range of fine climbing peaks was carved by glaciers from the Eolus Granite that has been dated at 1.46 billion years. Climbs usually center around a base camp in Chicago Basin that is accessed by trail from Needleton at mile **482.2**. The Needleton switch is at mile **483.9**, with a good view of Pigeon Peak just beyond to the right.

Ruby Creek enters the canyon at mile **484.6** along the contact of the Tenmile Granite, dated at 1.72 billion years, with the older metamorphic rocks. The contact is apparently along the eastward extension of the Coal Bank Pass fault. The northern contact of the Tenmile Granite with the metamorphic complex is at mile **488.9**. The slightly metamorphosed igneous intrusive body is named for Tenmile Creek that enters the canyon from the east at mile **487.3**.

At mile **489.6** a major fault crosses the Animas Canyon, juxtaposing sharply upturned beds of quartzite and slate of the Uncompahgre Formation to the north with the older metamorphic complex. These highly folded and thrust-faulted quartzites of an unknown Precambrian age comprise the Grenadier Range to the east, seen also from Molas Lake, and Snowdon Peak rising above Molas Pass to the west. The highly complex fault structures are graphically displayed along the canyon walls ahead. The tracks cross the Animas River at mile **489.9** north of the fault, and Elk Park at mile **490.5** is dominated by Mount Garfield (13,065 feet) at the west end of the Grenadiers. Glimpses of other peaks in the range—Graylock, Electric, Arrow, and Vestal—may be seen to the right as the train swings through Elk Park. These sharp peaks of very hard quartzite provide a mountaineer's delight. A major east-west fault at mile **491.6** is mapped from near Beartown some ten miles to the east, westward across the Animas Canyon to Molas Lake, where it disappears under lower Paleozoic sedimentary rocks. The north-bounding fault of the Grenadier fault complex is at mile **492** at the mouth of Whitehead Gulch, marked by a railroad waterspout. Here the quartzite is again faulted against the older Precambrian metamorphic complex. A small intrusive stock of Tenmile Granite is visible on the ridge to the north of Whitehead Gulch; dikes of the granite can be seen to cut the gneiss and schist near mile **493**.

A five-mile stretch of the narrow canyon from Elk Park to near Silverton is where severe damage has repeatedly occurred, mostly from heavy autumn rainstorms. Floods of 1895, 1911, and 1978 strewed twisted rails, weighing 30 pounds to the yard, as far downstream as Baker's Bridge.

At mile **496.1** the track crosses Mineral Creek just upstream from its confluence with the Animas and enters the open valleys that have been eroded from the margins of the Silverton caldera, a volcanic vent that is highly mineralized, especially along and near the borders, accounting for the many old mines and dumps visible in all quadrants. A view back down the Animas Canyon reveals that the canyon was cut in at least two stages. The upper U-shaped profile was carved by glacial erosion, later incised by a sharp stream-eroded V-shaped canyon at the bottom; this is some feat considering that the glaciers melted away only 10,000–15,000 years ago.

It is past lunchtime as we pull into Silverton at mile **496.7**. There will be plenty of time to feast and shop and live a little bit of history before The Silverton departs on the return trip. Since it is mid-summer, it will probably rain on the return trip to Durango. But it's all downhill from here!

Four Corners Region Place Names

A great many place names in the Four Corners region came from Spanish exploration parties who traversed the area several times in the sixteenth and seventeenth centuries. In many cases it is difficult to know who actually named which features, and in those situations where names seemed to appear from nowhere during the Spanish era, the Spanish explorers are credited. Among those responsible for many of the names, Coronado ca. 1540, Juan Maria Rivera in 1765, and the friars Silvestre Velez de Escalante and Francisco Antanasio Dominguez in 1776, were the most visible; certainly Escalante is the best known because of his journals.

Derivations and history behind these place names was taken from numerous sources. Many are from Spanish and Navajo language dictionaries, some are from guidebooks published by the New Mexico and Four Corners geological societies, some are intuitive for lack of definitely known origins, but the conclusions are explained.

Abajo. Spanish name meaning "lower" given by the Spanish explorers to the mountains of southeastern Utah because they are lower in elevation and/or farther south than the prominent La Sal Mountains in east-central Utah. The isolated intrusive igneous (laccolithic) range is known as the Blue Mountains or "The Blues" by local inhabitants.

Acoma Pueblo. Name derived from the Keresan Indian word *ako* meaning "white rock," and *ma* meaning "people." The village is situated on top of a mesa composed of the white Zuni Sandstone, capped by the Dakota Sandstone. It was mentioned by Fray Marcos de Niza in 1539, and Hernando de Alvarada visited the village in 1540. Acoma was captured by the Spaniards in a siege that lasted January 21–23, 1599. Acoma vies with the Hopi village of Oraibi in Arizona for being the oldest continually occupied city in the United States.

Agathla Peak or El Capitan. Peak composed of the neck of an ancient violently eruptive volcano (diatreme) north of Kayenta, Arizona. The name means "the place of the scraping of hides," a ritual site for communal sheepshearing, in Navajo language.

Albuquerque. New Mexico's colonial governor, don Francisco Cuervo y Valdez founded a villa in the Rio Grande valley in 1706, naming it San Francisco de Alburquerque in honor of don Francisco, Duque de Alburquerque and Viceroy of New Spain. The viceroy, fearful of offending King Philip V of Spain, renamed the villa San Felipe de Alburquerque for the king's patron saint. English-speaking people of the nineteenth century dropped the first "r," spelling it Albuquerque.

Aneth. Originally a trading post and now a village north of the San Juan River in extreme southeastern Utah. It has been impossible to trace the word as either a Navajo, Spanish, or family name. Regionally, the northern boundary of the Navajo Indian Reservation follows the center of the San Juan River as it occurred in 1868, but in this small corner of Utah the lands north of the river, historically homesteaded by Navajo families, were later added to the Reservation, and were known as the Annex lands. Since there has been a close association with the Spaniards and Mexicans, although not always amicable, for more than 200 years, many Spanish words with no Navajo counterparts have been included in the Navajo language. The Spanish word for annex is *anexo* (in this case the "x" is pronounced something like a soft "s"), perhaps pronounced in Navajo as "aneth." This is one explanation for the name.

Animas River. Name given by the Spanish explorers to the river in southwestern Colorado that flows from the high San Juan Mountains east of Silverton southward through Durango and into the San Juan River near Aztec, New Mexico, shortened from the original name Rio de las Animas Perdido, meaning "River of Lost Souls."

Apache. Spanish word for "thug," named by the Spanish explorers for the marauding bands of Indians they encountered in southern Arizona and New Mexico.

Arizona. From the Papago Indian word *arizonac,* meaning "place of the small spring" (*ali,* "small," and *shonak,* "place of the spring"), according to Will C. Barnes in *Arizona Place Names.* The Papago Nation is now called the Tohon O'Odham Nation. What is now southern Arizona was part of Sonora in the days of Spanish rule, and northern Arizona was part of New Mexico Territory. When the United States acquired the northern Sonoran lands with the Gadsden Purchase in 1853, the region became part of New Mexico. The name Arizonac was originally a station of the Saric Mission near important silver mines; the mining area was later called the District of Arizonac. The Spaniards soon dropped the "c" from the name, and Padre Ortega referred to the Real de Arizona as "the town in whose district were silver mines" in 1751; the village was destroyed by Spaniards ca. 1790. Arizona Territory was established by Congress on February 23, 1863, and John A. Gurley was appointed territorial governor by President Lincoln. Gurley died before traveling west of the Mississippi River, and his successor, John N. Goodwin, took the oath of office at Navajo Springs in the wilds of Arizona Territory on December 29, 1863. Arizona became the last of the 48 contiguous states on February 14, 1912.

Aztec. Town in northwestern New Mexico, settled in 1878 and incorporated in 1890, named for Aztec ruins which were erroneously believed to have been built by Indians related to the Aztecs of Mexico. The first commercial gas well in New Mexico was drilled within a half-mile of the townsite; Aztec was the first community in the state to use natural gas. Because gas pressures were not regulated in the early days, many homes burned to the ground as a result of fluctuating pressures that caused fires.

Belen. Spanish word for "Bethlehem," or "figures in Nativity scene," but colloquially means "bedlam, confusion, noise." The city south of Albuquerque, New Mexico, may have been named for the Spanish land grant of Nuestra Señora de Belen (Our Lady of Bethlehem) given to Spanish settlers by Governor Mendoza in 1740. Another possibility may be that the townsite was built on a village that had been destroyed by Indians during the Pueblo Revolt of 1860, and thus the reference to "bedlam."

Betatakin Ruin. An Anasazi (Navajo word for "ancient ones") cliff dwelling in Navajo National Monument in northeastern Arizona; name is Navajo for "ledge house." Discovered by Byron Cummings and John Wetherill in 1909.

Biklabito. Trading center near the northern Arizona-New Mexico border; name meaning "water under a rock" in the Navajo language.

Blanding. Town between Monticello and Bluff in southeastern Utah established by Mormon settlers and some religious and political refugees from Mexico in 1905.

Bluff. A town in southeastern Utah located on the north bank of the San Juan River that was settled by Mormon missionaries of the historic Hole-in-the-Rock migration from Cedar City and Kanab in 1880. Named for its location beneath massive, red sandstone cliffs, or bluffs.

Bondad. A trading stop midway between Aztec, New Mexico, and Durango, Colorado; word means "goodness" or "excellence" in Spanish.

Bright Angel Creek. A small, usually clear-water stream that drains the north rim of Grand Canyon, Arizona. Named by the John Wesley Powell river expedition in 1869, because they were pleased to find clean water entering the muddy Colorado River near mid-canyon, in sharp contrast to the Dirty Devil River upstream. Since that time, several features, such as the trail and hotel, have been given the name.

Cabezon. "Large head" in Spanish, an apt name for the large stone peak north of Albuquerque, New Mexico. It is the neck of an ancient volcano exhumed by erosion.

Cajone. Spanish for "large box."

Canyon de Chelly. This is a strange name for the red-rock canyon in the heart of Navajo country. Numerous historians have pondered the origin of the word without success. It is pronounced "de shay!" It seems to be a French word applied in Navajo country by Spaniards. Some have suggested it is a spelling corruption of the Navajo word *tsegi,* which means "rocky canyon," but this makes no sense linguistically to me.

I offer a more realistic explanation: In the early 1800s, the Navajos living in the canyon grew numerous peach trees, relying heavily on the crops for food. When Kit Carson tried rounding up the Navajos to put them on another reservation in 1864, he tried destroying their fields to starve them out of hiding. In so doing he cut down the peach trees in Cañon de Chelly, a Navajo stronghold since about 1700. In searching for a plausible origin of the name, it became obvious that the French word for "peach" is *pêche,* and "peach tree" is *pêcher.* A reasonable misunderstanding of pronunciation would easily make *pêche* or *pêcher* sound like "de-shay," or with a Spanish spelling for the sound: "de Chelly." The Frenchman who called the place Peach Canyon is long forgotten, and whoever tried to spell the sound in Spanish has long since disappeared, but it certainly seems logical that the French for Peach Canyon became present-day Canyon de Chelly. I hope that historians will consider this explanation, as all others have failed.

Canyon del Muerto. Tributary to Canyon de Chelly in Canyon de Chelly National Monument; name means "canyon of the dead" in Spanish. The name originated from the discovery of pre-historic Indian burials in the canyon by a Smithsonian Institution expedition led by James Stevenson in 1882. Another good reason for the name is that, following Navajo raids on Pueblo Indian villages and Spanish settlements in the Rio Grande Valley, a Spanish punitive expedition led by Lt. Antonio Narbona fought an extended battle with Navajos fortified in a rock cove (now known as Massacre Cave) in the canyon, reportedly killing 115 Navajos, including women and children.

Carrizo Mountains. Mountains in northeasternmost Arizona, west of the Lukachukai Mountains, name meaning "reed-grass" in Spanish.

Chama. Spanish for "barter, exchange."

Chinle. Village and trading center in Navajo Country at the mouth of Canyon de Chelly and the entrance to Canyon de Chelly National Monument. The name is Navajo for "at the mouth of the canyon," also translated as "place where the water flows out of the mountain." The original trading post was opened in 1882, and was operated from a tent by Naakaii Yazzie (Navajo for "Mexican Smith").

Chupadero. Spanish word for "sucking" or "absorbent," no doubt applied to the often dry riverbed in central New Mexico.

Chuska Mountains. In northwesternmost New Mexico; the name means "white spruce" in the Navajo language.

Colorado. Spanish word for "colored" or "red"; the name applied to the river by the Spanish explorers, namely Fr. Fransisco Garcés, who first saw the river in Grand Canyon. Prior to the construction of Glen Canyon Dam in 1963, the Colorado River often ran bright red through Grand Canyon due to the copious amounts of red sediments it carried. Since the dam was built, the river runs red only when there are floods in the Paria or Little Colorado drainage systems that enter the Colorado below the dam. The region around the headwaters of the Colorado River (formerly known as the Grand River from Granby Lake as far as the confluence with the Green River) was originally called Colorado Territory, later Colorado State.

Cortez. Named for Hernando Cortés, who conquered Mexico for Spain in 1519. The southwesternmost city in Colorado, Cortez is the county seat of Montezuma County, named for the native Mexican Indian chief conquered by Cortés.

Crested Butte. Originally a small supply center for the local gold and silver camps north of Gunnison, Colorado, it was founded in 1879 and named for the adjacent mountain of that descriptive name; now a popular ski resort.

Del Norte. Spanish words literally meaning "of the north."

Dinnehotso (Dennehotso). Trading post on the Navajo Indian Reservation 26 miles east of Kayenta, Arizona; name is Navajo for "peoples' farms."

Dirty Devil River. Named by the John Wesley Powell river expedition in 1869 for the tributary stream that enters the Colorado River near Hite, Utah. Dunn rowed his wooden river boat into the mouth of the stream and someone behind called out, "Is it a trout stream?" Dunn replied, "It's a dirty devil." The expedition, the first down the Colorado River, later found a clear stream entering near mid–Grand Canyon and named that one Bright Angel Creek in contrast.

Dolores. Spanish woman's given name applied by the Spanish explorers for the river in southwestern Colorado that drains the west side of the San Juan Mountains; later the name of the town built on the north bank of that river in 1877, incorporated in 1900. The word also means "sorrow" or "pain" in Spanish, probably the meaning conferred by the exploring Spaniards.

Dulce. Spanish word for "sweet" or "pleasant."

Durango. A Spanish word that generally means a small town, bigger than a pueblo but smaller than a ciudad. The Chamber of Commerce version is that the name was derived from the Basque word *urango*, meaning "water town" and that Durango was named by former territorial governor A.C. Hunt, who named it after Durango, Mexico, which in turn is named for Durango,

Spain. The town was known as Durango almost from the beginning; it was established in November, 1881, by the Denver & Rio Grande Railroad after negotiations failed with nearby Animas City for the site of their railroad hub. Animas City was later merged into the northern edge of Durango and lost its identity.

Estancia. A farming community in Torrence County, central New Mexico. The Spanish name means "large estate" or "resting place." Indeed, the settlement was founded by don Fernando Otero at Estancia Spring, a resting place for travelers on a trail from Santa Fe to Chihuahua, Mexico. Originally the area was known as Estancia Llano ("plain"), but it is now known as Estancia Valley.

Evacuation Creek. A polite name for the stream in west-central Colorado originally called Shit Creek.

Farmington. Town in northwestern New Mexico established in 1901 as an agricultural center.

Florida River. Spanish word meaning "flowery" or "choice."

Fort Defiance. Site of an army post established in 1851 to control the raiding activities of the Navajos and the headquarters for Kit Carson's roundup operations for "the long march" to Bosque Redondo, the Fort Sumner Indian Reservation, in 1864. After the return of the Navajos to their homelands, this was the site of the first trading post in Navajo country, established on August 28, 1868

Gallup. The town in northwestern New Mexico named for the paymaster of the Atlantic and Pacific Railroad (now known as the Santa Fe) in 1882. Formerly a coal distribution center, the town is now sometimes referred to as the Indian Capitol of the Southwest. It is a trading center for the Navajo, who live on their reservation to the north, and the Zuni Indians to the south.

Gateway. A village in west-central Colorado at the mouth of Unaweap Canyon. It was the site of a supply camp for the U.S. Geological and Geographical Survey (the Hayden Survey) parties in 1875. At an elevation of 4,595 feet, it is the lowest settlement in western Colorado.

Glenwood Springs. The town, at the confluence of the Colorado and Roaring Fork rivers in north-central Colorado, was founded in 1882 by the Defiance Town and Land Company. They intended to exploit the supposed curative powers of the hot springs located here, long used by the Ute Indians to cure aches and pains of both people and animals. The infamous John Henry "Doc"

Holliday came here for the "miraculous healing powers" of the hot mineral springs, but died of tuberculosis in 1887 and was buried here.

Gobernador. Spanish word meaning "governor."

Goulding's Trading Post. Trading Post, Motel, and Navajo boarding school near Monument Valley in northeastern Arizona. Harry Goulding came to Monument Valley in 1923 and established the trading post for Navajo trade, building the stone structure in 1927 and adding the first tourist quarters in 1928–29. He made Monument Valley famous when in the 1930s he coaxed Hollywood film producers into making western movies here, mostly starring John Wayne.

Granada. Trading post and mission in Navajo country near the intersection of Arizona Highways 63 and 264 west of Window Rock, Arizona. Name means "cattle" in Spanish. The Hubbell Trading Post, established in 1876 by John Lorenzo Hubbell, was designated a National Historic Site in February, 1967, to preserve a realistic picture of the old Navajo trading days.

Grand Junction. City in west-central Colorado named because it is located at the confluence of the Colorado River (formerly "Grand") and the Gunnison River. The "Grand River" joins with the Green River to form the Colorado River below the confluence. The name was formally changed to "Colorado" above the confluence by an act of the Colorado State Legislature on March 24, 1921, and by an act of Congress approved July 25, 1921. The townsite was selected on September 26, 1881, following the opening of the region for settlement after the Ute Indians had been removed to reservations on September 4, 1881. The town, now the largest between Denver and Salt Lake City, was incorporated on June 22, 1882.

Grants, New Mexico. This favorite off-reservation trading center for the Navajos, also a mining, lumbering, and ranching center, is named for the Grant brothers (Augustus, Lewis, and John), who were railroad construction contractors and maintained a camp for railroad workers here known as Grants Camp. The site was later a coaling station for the Atcheson, Topeka, and the Santa Fe Railroad known as Grants Station.

Green River. The name originated in Spanish. The early Spanish explorers called the river in eastern Utah the San Buenaventura, believing that it flowed westward into the Great Basin country of western Utah. However, it was later realized that the river flows southward through northeastern Utah to join with the Colorado River, and it was renamed the Rio Verde, later translated into English as the Green River. Opinions differ as to the original meaning of the descriptor "green." Some think it was because of the green vegetation that lined the river's banks in an otherwise drab, barren countryside; others think it was named for the color of the water. After viewing the color of the water for many years in various seasons, I favor the former interpretation. The name is also applied to two cities, one in south-central Wyoming near the headwaters; the other in east-central Utah located at the site of a popular river crossing, known as Gunnison Crossing, and the crossing of the river by the Union Pacific Railroad.

Gunnison. Town founded in 1874 at the junction of the Gunnison River and Tomichi Creek in the central Colorado Rocky Mountains. The town became popular during the mining rush of 1879–80, but nearly died after the silver panic of 1893. It was rejuvenated during the recreational boom of the 1960s and 1970s, and is the home of Western Colorado State University and gateway to the Crested Butte ski resort. Named for Captain Gunnison.

Gunnison River. Formerly known as the Rio Javier or the Indian name Tomichi, it was renamed the Gunnison after the death of Captain Gunnison in the fall of 1853.

Hovenweep National Monument. Reserved for scattered, mostly surface Anasazi Indian ruins in southwestern Colorado on May 2, 1923; name is Ute Indian for "deserted valley."

Huerfano. Spanish word for "orphan."

Isleta Pueblo. Spanish name for a "village" built on a "little island" surrounded by the Rio Grande floodplain. The original pueblo was located on the present-day site when Coronado visited this area in 1540. Raids by Plains Indians caused Pueblo Indians living east of the Manzano Mountains to move here around 1675. The Isleta Pueblo did not participate in the Pueblo Revolt against the Spaniards in 1680, but Governor Otermin captured 400–500 prisoners from Isleta in 1681. Others living in the pueblo escaped to Hopi country in Arizona, returning in 1716 with Hopi relatives. Residents of Acoma and Laguna moved to Isleta in the early 1800s as a result of droughts and religious problems, thus Isleta is a community of a variety of migrants.

Joyita. Small jewel.

Kayenta. Trading center on the Navajo Indian Reservation in northeastern Arizona, originally a trading post operated by John and

Louisa Wetherill, founded in 1910. The location was originally called Todanestya (Navajo meaning "where water runs like fingers out of a hill"), later changed to Kayenta, an Anglo corruption of the Navajo word Tyende ("where the animals bog down"). John Wetherill made significant archeological discoveries of Mesa Verde, now a National Park, and Betatakin, Keet Seel, and Inscription House ruins, now in Navajo National Monument, and was the first white man to see Rainbow Bridge. Kayenta, pronounced something like a sloppy "kanta" by local people, was once known as "the farthest place from anything" in the United States.

Ladron Mountains. Spanish word for "thief" or "robber."

La Junta. Spanish word for "board," as in a governing board.

La Plata. Spanish word for "silver," named by Spanish explorers led by Juan Maria Rivera in 1765, who found silver minerals in the mountain range. La Plata County, formed in 1874 with Parrot City as the county seat (Durango is now the county seat), was named for the mineral-rich laccolithic range.

La Sal. Spanish word for "salt," the name given to the mountain range in east-central Utah by the Spanish explorers. The name is most appropriate, as the mountains were formed by igneous intrusions into thick, salt flowage structures in middle Tertiary time. How the Spaniards knew the relationships of the mountains to the completely subsurface occurrence of salt is a mystery, but there have been unconfirmed reports of saltwater springs in these mountains. Also, saltwater springs along the Dolores River in Paradox Valley south of the range could have been the tipoff.

Lucero Mountains. Spanish word meaning "morning star" or "splendor."

Lukachukai Mountains. Mountains in northwesternmost New Mexico, north of Chuska Mountains; name means "place of slender reeds" in the Navajo language.

Mamm Creek. Polite name given to a creek east of Grand Junction, Colorado, originally known as Tit Creek.

Mancos. Spanish word for those who are "armless," "defective," or "faulty." The reason for the Spanish explorers to apply this term to the Mancos River and later the town of Mancos is probably because the river has no major tributaries.

Manzano. Spanish word for "apple trees," which grew in two orchards near the village on the east slope of the Manzano Mountains, southeast of Albuquerque, New Mexico. The trees were originally believed to have been planted during the Spanish missionary period before 1676, but dating of the growth rings of the trees has established that they were planted no longer ago than 1800.

Mesa Verde. A descriptive term used by the Spanish explorers for the "green tableland" between Mancos and Cortez in southwestern Colorado. The high wilderness region was the homelands of Ute Indians in the mid-1800s, and white settlers avoided the region. The first discovery of Anasazi ruins was reported by W.H. Jackson, photographer for the U.S. Geological and Geographical Survey, who photographed the region in 1874. However, the discovery of Cliff Palace by two cowboys, Richard Wetherill and Charlie Mason, in December, 1888, brought notoriety to the region. It was established as a National Park on June 29, 1906, to display and preserve Anasazi Indian artifacts.

Mexican Hat. Village in southeastern Utah located on the San Juan River north of Monument Valley, named for a monolith near the town that is shaped like a conical peak, capped by a very large, round, balanced rock, giving the appearance of a dozing Mexican wearing a sombrero. The town was originally known as Goodridge, named for the turn-of-the-century prospector who discovered shallow oil at the site in 1908. The Mexican Hat townsite was then located about 1.5 miles to the north; Mexican Hat was abandoned in 1930, and the name was transferred to the present site. The Mexican Hat Field still produces oil in barely economical quantities; miniature pump-jacks can be seen scattered around the countryside in and near the town.

Mexican Water. Trading Post on the Navajo Indian Reservation in northeastern Arizona, known as Naki-Toh ("traveler's water") in Navajo; the freshwater springs emanating from the Navajo Sandstone have been used by travelers for decades, perhaps centuries.

Moab. Name of the town in east-central Utah given by the Mormon settlers; from an ancient biblical kingdom east of the Red Sea, in what is now Jordan.

Molas Lake. Scenic alpine lake south of Silverton, Colorado, in the heart of the San Juan Mountains. The name is Spanish for "moles" but marmots are what commonly dot the lakeshore areas with burrow mounds. (Correctly pronounced "mole!-us.")

Monticello. Town in southeastern Utah established by Mormon settlers from Bluff, Utah, in 1886.

Mount Taylor. Coronado passed Mount Taylor in 1540 on his way to Acoma and mentioned the volcanic features in the area. The ancient volcanic cone was known variously as Sierra San Mateo and Cebolleta ("tender onion") to the Spaniards, and Dtzo Dzil, the sacred mountain guarding the southern boundary of Navajo country, to the Navajos. Simpson, working on transcontinental railroad rights-of-way in 1850, named the mountain after the president.

Nacimiento Mountains. Name is the Spanish word for "birth, nativity, origin."

Navajo. Name given to the local Indians living in the general region of the present-day San Juan Basin by the Spanish explorers. The origin of the name is in doubt, for it has several meanings. Some historians believe the name was derived from a Tewa-speaking Pueblo Indian place called "navaju," which is believed to have meant "large area of cultivated lands"; however, the modern Spanish word *navajo* means either "plain" or "stupid." We prefer to think that the arrogant Spanish explorers referred to the Indians as "plain," or unsophisticated, people.

Navajo Mountain. High monolithic landmark east of Lake Powell in northeastern Arizona. It is called Not is Ahn or "place of the enemies" by Navajos.

Nazlini Wash. A prominent canyon and wash south of Canyon de Chelly in Navajo country; name is Navajo for "flows in a crescent shape," also translated "runs crooked."

Ouray. The town between Silverton and Montrose in southwestern Colorado and another near Vernal, Utah, named for the Ute Indian chief, a great friend of the white people. Pronounced "your!-ray" in southwestern Colorado, but the village in northeastern Utah is pronounced "oh!-ray." The village in Colorado was originally called Uncompahgre for the stream that flows through town, a Ute Indian word meaning "warm stream," because being fed by hot springs, the stream never freezes in winter. Ouray, Colorado, was incorporated and given its present name in 1876.

Paradox. Name of a village and long valley in west-central Colorado. The valley, which extends into easternmost Utah, is the collapsed top of a salt-flowage structure, known as a salt anticline; a deep well drilled into the valley penetrated nearly 15,000 feet of salt and closely related sedimentary rock. The Dolores River crosses the structurally controlled valley at nearly right angles, rather than flowing down the valley as other rivers do. The course of the river had been established on a surface far above the present-day land level, and regional erosion removed the overburden from the salt structure. When the riverbed cut down to the top of the northwest-trending elongate structure, the river was hopelessly trapped in its canyon and actually cut across the structure. Subsequent erosion and collapse of the salt anticline formed the present-day valley. Seeing this as a most unusual situation, pioneers in the region named it Paradox Valley, and the village also took that name. The usually deeply buried salt strata were named the Paradox Formation, and the ancient basin in which the salt was deposited was named the Paradox Basin. A popular T-shirt available in the area asks the burning question, "Where in the hell is Paradox?" The answer is on the back, "Right next to Bedrock."

Paria River. The word is Spanish for "pariah" or "outcast."

Piceance. Polite name given to a topographic and geologic basin in north-central Colorado as a French-like spelling of the original name, Piss Ants Basin.

Piedra. Spanish for "stone, gravel."

Piedra River. Spanish for "stone" or "gravel," perhaps best translated as "rocky river."

Pine River. Originally named the Rio Piños by the Spanish explorers; now known by the English translation.

Redondo. Spanish for "round."

Rio Grande. Spanish term for "Grand River," often misused in English as the "Rio Grande River," which literally means "River Grande River."

Rio Puerco. Spanish name meaning "Dirty River" or "Pig River," an apt descriptive name for the central New Mexico intermittent stream.

Salida. Spanish word for "exit," also meaning "start." The town in central Colorado named for its location with respect to the exit (or entrance) to the Rocky Mountains via the canyon of the Arkansas River; mispronounced in Colorado as "Sal-eye!-da."

Sandia. Spanish word for "watermelon," named for the sliced watermelon-like appearance of the Sandia Mountains.

San Juan. Name meaning Saint John given to the river and mountain range in southwestern Colorado by the Spanish explorers, probably Juan Maria Rivera in 1765.

Santa Fe. Name given to the Spanish government city in north-central New Mexico in 1610, the name meaning "Saint of Faith." The city has since been the site of the Spanish, Mexican, U.S. Military, and State capitols.

Ship Rock. Name given to the prominent monolith in northeasternmost New Mexico and the nearby town for the sailing-ship appearance of the rock, which rises 1,800 feet from a nearly flat and barren plain. The monolith is the remains of a diatreme, the preserved neck of a blowout volcano. Ship Rock is considered a holy place by Navajo Indians, who call it Tse Bitai ("the winged rock").

Silverton. Name of the village in the heart of the San Juan Mountains that was a mining center (mostly for silver) in the late 1800s. Modern, sporadic mining operations in the area are mainly for gold. The first year-round settlers arrived in about 1874. The initial settlement was named Baker's Park for Charles Baker, who led a party of prospectors into the area in 1860–61. The party was harassed by Ute Indians and heavy snows, and escaped southward to near the site of Baker's Bridge north of Durango. This was the first group of whites to have visited the site of present-day Durango. Baker was later killed by the Indians.

Socorro. Spanish for "HELP!" Actually a shortened form of the Virgin Mary's title, Our Lady of Perpetual Help.

Taos. Town in north-central New Mexico. The Spanish "taos" means the badges of the orders of Saint Anthony and Saint John.

Teec nos pos. The site of the original trading post on the Navajo Reservation in northeasternmost Arizona, known by its Navajo name, meaning "circle of seven cottonwood trees."

Telluride. A general mineralogical term indicating a metal, such as gold or silver, that rarely occurs in combination with tellurium. An example is hessite, Ag_2Te. In the 1880s, such tellurides were found in mines near this west-central Colorado mining town.

Tes Nez Iah Trading Post. Trading center 39.5 miles east of Kayenta, Arizona, on U.S. Highway 160 in Navajo Country; name is Navajo for "tall cottonwood grove."

Tijeras Canyon. Spanish word for "scissors," and the canyon directly east of Albuquerque certainly appears to be a scissors cut between the Sandia (watermelon) Mountains to the north and the Manzano (apple) Mountains to the south.

Tonto (Tonto Plateau). Spanish for "fool" or "stupid."

Torreon. This village was given the Spanish name for "towers" built as fortifications to guard against attacks by Apache Indians.

Tsalie. Trading center on the Navajo Indian Reservation 20 miles east of Many Farms in northeastern Arizona; name is Navajo for "flows into the rocks."

Tsegi Trading Post. Trading post 11.4 miles southwest of Kayenta on U.S. Highway 160; name is Navajo for "rock Canyon," and not surprisingly, it is in a rocky canyon.

Tuba City. Founded by Mormons in 1872, who named it for Tueve, a Hopi leader from Oraibi, whose name the Mormons mispronounced. The government bought them out in 1903 to establish Tuba City as an Indian Bureau headquarters. The Tuba Trading Post, built of native stone in 1905 in the circular shape of a Navajo hogan, is still in business today near the Navajo Reservation's only McDonald's, Taco Bell, and Dairy Queen eating establishments.

Unaweap Canyon. A large, broad-bottomed canyon that crosses the Uncompahgre Plateau, traversed by Colorado Highway 141. Tiny streams drain the huge canyon, both northward into the Gunnison River and to the south into the Dolores River near Gateway, Colorado. It is believed that the oversized canyon was the original route of the Gunnison River before it was diverted toward the north by stream capture. The name is a Ute Indian word meaning "canyon with two mouths."

Uncompahgre River. Flowing north from the San Juan Mountains of southwestern Colorado, the river passes through Ouray, where it is fed by hot springs. The name is said to be a corruption of the Ute Indian word *ancapogari* meaning "red lake." The Utes gave the river that name because near its source was a spring of hot, reddish water, disagreeable to the taste. Other translations include "warm-running river" and other similar meanings.

Uravan. A contraction of the mineral names "uranium" and "vanadium," it is a company town for Union Carbide, a company that mined and processed ores of those minerals in this area in the 1940s and 1950s.

Utah. Named for a tribe of Indians, the Utes, who dominated mountainous regions of the southern Rocky Mountains when white settlers arrived. The name is from the Spanish *uta* given to the Native Americans by the early Spanish explorers, the word meaning "pimple-faced."

Glossary

Angular Unconformity. An unconformity or break between two series of rock layers such that rocks of the lower series underlie rocks of the upper series at an angle; the two series are not parallel. The lower series was deposited, then tilted and eroded prior to deposition of the upper layers.

Anticline. An elongate fold in the rocks in which sides slope downward and away from the crest; an upfold.

Arkose. A sandstone containing a significant proportion of feldspar grains, usually signifying a source area composed of granite or gneiss.

Base Level. The level, actual or potential, toward which erosion constantly works to lower the land. Sea level is the general base level, but there may be local, temporary base levels such as lakes.

Basement. In geology, the crust of the earth beneath sedimentary deposits, usually, but not necessarily, consisting of metamorphic and/or igneous rocks of Precambrian age.

Basement Fault. A fault that displaces basement rocks and originated prior to deposition of overlying sedimentary rocks. Such faults may or may not extend upward into overlying strata, depending upon their history of rejuvenation.

Bentonite. A rock composed of clay minerals and derived from the alteration of volcanic tuff or ash.

Brachiopod. A type of shelled marine invertebrate now relatively rare but abundant in earlier periods of earth history. They are common fossils in rocks of Paleozoic age. Brachiopods have a bivalve shell that is symmetrical right and left of center.

Bryozoa. Tiny aquatic animals that build large colonial structures that are common as fossils in rocks of Paleozoic age.

Carbon 14 Dating or **Radiocarbon Dating.** A method of determining an age in years by measuring the concentration of carbon-14 remaining in formerly living matter, based on the assumption that assimilation of carbon-14 ceased abruptly at the time of death and that it thereafter remained a closed system. A half-life of 5,570 ($\pm$30) years for carbon-14 makes the method useful in determining ages in the range of 500–40,000 years.

Chert. A very dense siliceous rock usually found as nodular or concretionary masses, or as distinct beds, associated with limestones. **Jasper** is red chert containing iron-oxide impurities.

Cirque. Semicircular, bowl-shaped valley, usually perched high on a mountainside; formed by the plucking action of ice at the head of alpine glaciers

Clastic rocks. Deposits consisting of fragments of preexisting rocks; conglomerate, sandstone, and shale are examples.

Conglomerate. The consolidated equivalent of gravel. The constituent rock and mineral fragments may be of varied composition and range widely in size. The rock fragments are rounded and smoothed from transportation by water.

Contact. The surface, often irregular, which constitutes the junction of two bodies of rock.

Continental Deposits. Deposits laid down on land or in bodies of water not connected with the ocean.

Correlation. The process of determining the position or time of occurrence of one geologic phenomenon in relation to others. Usually it means determining the equivalence of geologic formations in separated areas through a comparison and study of fossils or rock peculiarities.

Crinoid. Marine invertebrate animals, abundant as fossils in rocks of Paleozoic age. Most lived attached to the bottom by a jointed stalk, the "head" resembling a lily-like plant, hence the common name "sea lily."

Dike. A sheetlike body of igneous rock that filled a fissure in older rock while in a molten state. Dikes that intrude layered rocks cut the beds at an angle.

Disconformity. A break in the orderly sequence of stratified rocks above and below which the beds are parallel. The break is usually indicated by erosional channels, indicating a lapse of time or absence of part of the rock sequence.

Dolomite. A mineral composed of calcium and magnesium carbonate, $(Ca,Mg)CO_3$, or a rock composed chiefly of the mineral dolomite, formed by alteration of limestone.

Dome. An upfold in which strata dip downward in all directions from a central area; the opposite of a basin.

Drumlin. A low, smoothly rounded, elongated and oval hill, mound, or ridge of compact glacial till (moraine), built under the margin of the ice and shaped by its flow; its longer axis is parallel to the flow direction, and its blunt end points in the direction from which the ice approached.

Eolian. Pertaining to wind. Designates rocks or soils whose constituents have been transported and deposited by wind. Windblown sand and dust (loess) deposits are termed "eolian."

Erosional Unconformity. A break in the continuity of deposition of a series of rocks caused by an episode of erosion.

Extrusive Rock. A rock that has solidified from molten material poured or thrown out onto the earth's surface by volcanic activity.

Facies. Generally, the term refers to a physical aspect or characteristic of a sedimentary rock, as related to adjacent strata. It is usually applied to distinguish different aspects of the sediments in time-equivalent or laterally continuous beds. For example, the white sandstone facies of the Cedar Mesa Sandstone changes laterally to the age-equivalent red arkosic sandstone facies of the Cutler Group in Canyonlands Country. Such a change from one aspect to another is called a **facies change.**

Fault. A break or fracture in rocks, along which there has been movement, one side relative to the other. Displacement along a fault may be vertical (**normal** or **reverse fault**) or lateral (**strike–slip** or **wrench fault**).

Foraminifera. Generally microscopic, one-celled animals (Protozoa), almost entirely of marine origin, with sufficiently durable shells capable of being preserved as fossils. They are usually abundant in marine sediments, and are sufficiently small to be retrievable in drill cuttings and cores.

Formation. The fundamental unit in the local classification of layered rocks, consisting of a bed or beds of similar or closely related rock types and differing from strata above and below. A formation must be readily distinguishable, thick enough to be mapped, and of broad regional extent. A formation may be subdivided into two or more **members**, and/or combined with other closely related formations to form a **group**.

Geologic Map. A map showing the geographic distribution of geologic formations and other geologic features, such as folds, faults, and mineral deposits, by means of color or other appropriate symbols.

Glacier. A large mass of ice formed by the compaction and recrystallization of snow, moving slowly by creep downslope due to the stress of its own weight and surviving from year to year.

Gneiss. A banded metamorphic rock with alternating layers of usually tabular, unlike minerals.

Granite. An intrusive igneous rock with visibly granular, interlocking, crystalline quartz, feldspar, and perhaps other minerals.

Granogabbro. A rare form of granodiorite that contains more than 50% plagioclase feldspar; granodiorite is a coarse-grained intrusive igneous rock, generally intermediate in composition between granite and diorite in terms of quartz and feldspar content.

Horn. A high, rocky, pyramidal mountain peak with prominent faces and ridges, bounded by the intersecting walls of three or more cirques that have been cut back into a mountain by headward erosion of glaciers.

Igneous Rock. Rocks formed by solidification of molten material **(magma),** including rocks crystallized from cooling magma at depth **(intrusive),** and those poured out onto the surface as lavas **(extrusive)**.

Intrusive Rock. Rock that has solidified from molten material within the earth's crust and did not reach the surface; usually has a visibly crystalline texture.

Limestone. A bedded sedimentary deposit consisting chiefly of calcium carbonate, $CaCO_3$, usually formed from the calcified hard parts of organisms.

Lineament. A term generally applied to very long or slightly curved features on the earth's surface commonly associated with faults or fault zones.

Massif. A massive topographic and structural uplift, commonly formed of rocks more rigid than those of its surroundings. These rocks are commonly protruding bodies of basement rocks, consolidated during earlier orogenies.

Metamorphic Rock. Rocks formed by the alteration of preexisting igneous or sedimentary rocks, usually by intense heat and/or pressure, or mineralizing fluids.

Moraine. A mound, ridge, or other distinct accumulation of unsorted, unstratified drift, predominantly a heterogeneous mixture of mud, sand, gravel, and boulders, deposited by the melting of glacial ice.

Nunatak. An isolated hill or peak of bedrock that projects prominently above the surface of a glacier and is completely surrounded by glacial ice.

Oolitic. A descriptive term applied to a rock, usually limestone, containing a proportion of ooliths: rounded sand-size grains, usually composed of calcium carbonate, formed of concretionary layers added to the outside of a nuclear grain such as a shell fragment or lime pellet in a shallow, high-energy environment of deposition. From the Greek *oon*, "egg"; pronounced oh-oh litic.

Orogeny. Literally, the process of formation of mountains, but practically it refers to the processes by which structures in mountainous regions were formed, including folding, thrusting, and faulting in the outer layers of the crust, and plastic folding, metamorphism and plutonism (emplacement of magmas) in the inner layers. An episode of structural deformation may be called an orogeny, e.g., the Laramide Orogeny.

Sandstone. A consolidated rock composed of sand grains cemented together; usually composed predominantly of quartz, it may contain other sand-size fragments of rocks and/or minerals.

Schist. A crystalline metamorphic rock with closely spaced foliation **(platy)** that splits into thin flakes or slabs.

Sedimentary Rock. Rocks composed of sediments, usually aggregated through processes of water, wind, glacial ice, or organisms, derived from preexisting rocks, or in the case of limestones, constituent particles are usually derived from organic processes.

Shale. Solidified muds, clays, and silts that are fissile (split like paper) and break along original bedding planes.

Sill. A tabular body of igneous rock that was injected in the molten state concordantly between layers of preexisting rocks.

Stratigraphy. The definition and interpretation of the layered rocks, the conditions of their formation, their character, arrangements, sequence, age, distribution, and correlation, using fossils and other means.

Stratum. A single layer of sedimentary rock, separated from adjacent strata by surfaces of erosion, non-deposition, or abrupt changes in character. Plural **strata.**

Syncline. An elongate, troughlike downfold in which the sides dip downward and inward toward the axis.

Tarn. A relatively small and deep pool occupying an ice-gouged rock basin, usually at the bottom of a cirque.

Tectonic. Pertaining to rock structures formed by earth movements, especially those that are widespread.

Trilobite. A general term for a group of extinct animals (arthropods) that occurs as fossils in rocks of Paleozoic age. They consist of flattened, segmented shells with a distinct thoraxial lobe and paired appendages; usually found as partial fragments.

Type Locality. The place from which the name of a geologic formation is taken and where the unique characteristics of the formation may be examined.

Unconformity. A surface of erosion or nondeposition separating sequences of layered rocks.

Index

Baker, Charles, 94, 124
Baker's Bridge, 84, 94, 124, 127
Bakers Bridge Granite: seen from train, 155; tour site for, 124
basement rocks, 6, 7, 18–34 passim, 51, 59, 66, 74, 128, 141, 147, 150; climbing, 107, 111; tour sites for, 124, 129, 133, and views of, 130
Bear Creek Falls: tour site for, 142
Beartown, 139, 157
bentonite, 69
Big Bear Creek, 113
Bilk Creek Sandstone, 146
Bluff Sandstone, 68
Boomerang Road, 147
Box Canyon: climbing, 111, 112; tour site for, 143; viewing, 42, 44
brachiopods, 35, 36, 41; tour site for, 131
Bradshaw, Charles, 153
Bull Lake glacial epoch, 83, 119

cactolith, 137
calderas, 75, 76; tour sites for, 140, 141
California comparisons, 21, 23, 24
Cambrian System, 10, 13, 35–38, 144; climbing and, 106; seen from train, 155; tour sites for, 125, 130, 131, 135. See also Ignacio Formation
Camp Bird Mine, 112
campgrounds, 111, 141, 143, 147
campsites, climbing, 111, 112, 114, 156
carbon dating, 83

Carboniferous System, 10, 47
Cascade Creek, 36, 156; tour sites for, 126, 129, 130, 137; viewing, 40
Cenozoic Era, 12, 13. See also Quaternary and Tertiary
Central Colorado Trough, 49
Chicago Basin, 108
Chicago Bridge, 156
Chief Ouray, 144
Chinle Formation, 66
Cimarron Creek, 115
Cinnamon Pass, 114
cirques, 81, 85; tour site for viewing, 138
Cleveland-Lloyd Quarry, 68
Cliffhouse Sandstone, 71, 152
clink : clunk ratio, 83
coal, 71
Coal Bank Pass, *Plate 9;* 28, 125, 126, 127, 150; climbing, 102, 104; tour sites for, 130, 133–34, 135; viewing, 40, 44, 54, 80
Cola Bank (Pass) fault, 28, 37, 42, 54, 57, 150, 156; climbing, 102–3, 107; tour site view of, 134
College Hill, 119, 121
Colorado, 91
Colorado National Monument, 66, 68
Colorado Plateau, 6, 59, 67, 68, 74
conglomerates, 12, 26, 37, 39, 57, 61, 71, 74; climbing, 103, 106; tour sites for, 125, 133–35, 137, 144
conodonts, 41
contact zones, 137, 150, 151, 152, 156, 157

Hermosa Mountain, 50, 52, 54, 61; seen from Durango, 121, from train, 154; tour sites for, 123, 124
Hesperas, 124
highway tour overview, 117–19
Hogback fault, 30
hogback ridges, 71; seen from Durango, 122
Holmes, William Henry, 90
Honaker Trail Formation, 52, 54; tour site for, 123
horns, 81, 82, 108, 111, 112, 115, 141
horsts, 20
hot springs: tour site for, 144
House Creek fault, 30
Howe, Ernest, 91

Ice Age, 79, 138. *See also* glaciers
Ice Cap, San Juan, 80. *See also* glaciers
Ice Lake Basin, 111
Idarado Mining Company, 141
Iddings, Joseph P., 93
Ignacio Formation, 36, 37; seen from train, 155; tour sites for, 125, 128, 130, 131, 133, 135, 139–40
Ignacio Reservoir, 128
igneous rock, 12, 27, 74, 77, 93; climbing, 104, 112, 113, and viewing, 111; contact zone for, 137; laccolithic, 152; seen from Durango, 122; tour sites for, 124, 131, 137, and viewing, 144. *See also* extrusive igneous rock *and* intrusive igneous rock
interbedded rock layers, 15
intrusive igneous rock, 27, 76,

77, 104; seen from train, 156; tour sites for, 124, 128, 131, 140, and viewing, 147, 148, 152
Ironton, 140, 142
Ironton Park, 81, 82, 142
Irving, J. D., 91
Irving Greenstone, 26

J-2 Unconformity, 67
Johannsen, Albert, 91
Junction Creek Sandstone, 67; seen from Durango, 121, from train, 154; tour site for, 123
Jurassic Period, 12, 13, 66, 68, 73; seen from Durango, 121, 122, from train, 154; tour site for, 123, and viewing, 145

Kaibab Uplift, 73
karst surface, 46
karst towers, 45; tour view of, 139
Kendall Mountain, 75, 81
Keystone Hill: tour site for, 146
kimberlite, 131
Kirtland Fruitland Formation, 71
Kismet Peak, 112

Lake Animas, 84
Lake City, 5, 80, 114, 114, 142
Lake City caldera, 76
Lake City West Group, 113–14
Lake Fork of the Gunnison River, 114
landslides: tour sites for, 143, 147, and viewing, 148
La Plata (Mountain) Range, 74, 77, 89, 104, 121, 122, 151, 152
Lapworth, Charles, 10
Laramide orogeny, 73, 74

Precambrian Era, 11, 13, 18–34, 75, 124, 128, 129, 133–34, 137, 138, 142, 143, 144, 155; climbing, 107, 108, 110, 111, 112, and viewing, 104, 104, 106; seen from train, 155, 156; tour sites for, 124, 127

precious ore, 77. *See also* gold

prospectors, 94. *See also* mining

Purgatory Ski Area, 28, 36, 46, 102, 108, 126, 128

pyrite, 150

Quantitative Classification of Igneous Rocks, 93

quartzites, 26, 37, 39, 41, 111, 112; climbing, 110, 111, 112, and viewing, 104, 106; tour sites for, 125, 130, 133–35, 137, 138, 142, 143, 144, 145

Quaternary Period, 12, 13. *See also* glaciers *and* moraines

radioactive minerals, 17, 27

railroads, 5, 95, 108, 128, 140–41, 148, 151, 153

Redcloud Peak, 90, 113, 114

Red Mountain Pass, 81, 140, 147; tour site for, 141

red rocks, 59, 103; seen from Durango, 121, from train, 154; tour site for, 123, and viewing, 133, 138, 143, 146, 151

reef, ancient: tour site for, 143

Rhoda, Franklin, 90

Richardson, Floyd, 114

Rico, 56, 63, 113, 117, 149, 150

Rico dome: tour sites for, 149, 150, 151

Rico Formation: tour site for, 150

Ridgeway, 49, 82, 111, 117, 145

Ridgeway fault: tour site for viewing, 145

Rio Grande, 4, 89, 94

Rio Grande Pyramid, 90

Rio Grande Southern Railroad, 148

ripple marks, 32; tour sites for, 142, 143

Rivera, Juan Maria de, 89

rock categories, 12, 14

rock climbing, 108, 110, 138; guide to, 102

rock glaciers, 85, 104, 113

Rockwood, 128, 154, 155

Rockwood Quarry, 46; seen from train, 155; tour site for, 126

Rocky Mountain Boom Time: A History of Durango, 95

Rocky Mountains, 6, 59, 68, 74

Ross, C. S., 91

Rotary Park, 144

Ruby Creek, 109; seen from train, 156

Ruffner, E. H., 90

salt, 40, 49, 52, 54, 127, 131, 170

sandstone, 12, 13, 15, 26, 37, 38, 50, 53, 54, 61, 66, 69; tour site for, 137. *See also* McCracken Sandstone Member *and separately by name*

Sandstone Mountain: tour site for, 150

sanidine trachyte porphory: tour site for, 137

San Jose Formation, 74

wrench fault, 20–25, 37, 41, 42, 48, 49, 55–56, 61–64; climbing, 110; tour site for, 135

X-Rock, 67

Yankee Boy Basin, 112, 144
Yoder, H. S., Jr., 93
Yount, George C., 90
yo-yo fault, 21, 37

Zuni Sandstone, 160